CATHOLICISM
IN DIALOGUE

General Editor: Robert A. Ludwig

Sheed & Ward's **Catholic Studies Series** presents reader-friendly texts to college classrooms and the broader community of faith and learning. Authored by scholars committed to both solid academic content and the lived experience of faith today, the books in the series are interdisciplinary and represent the Catholic heritage in all its richness. Consistent with Sheed & Ward's distinguished history, these books promise quality, character, and an approach to the Catholic experience that is in tune with the signs of the times.

CATHOLICISM IN DIALOGUE

Conversations across Traditions

WAYNE TEASDALE

A SHEED & WARD BOOK

ROWMAN & LITTLEFIELD PUBLISHERS, INC.
Lanham • Boulder • New York • Oxford

A SHEED & WARD BOOK

ROWMAN & LITTLEFIELD PUBLISHERS, INC.

Published in the United States of America
by Rowman & Littlefield Publishers, Inc.
A wholly owned subsidiary of The Rowman & Littlefield Publishing Group, Inc.
4501 Forbes Boulevard, Suite 200, Lanham, Maryland 20706
www.rowmanlittlefield.com

PO Box 317
Oxford
OX2 9RU, UK

British Library Cataloguing in Publication Information Available

Library of Congress Cataloging-in-Publication Data

Teasdale, Wayne.
　Catholicism in dialogue : conversations across traditions /
Wayne Teasdale.
　　p. cm. — (Sheed & Ward Catholic studies series)
　Includes bibliographical references and index.
　ISBN 0-7425-3177-5 (alk. paper)—ISBN 0-7425-3178-3 (pbk. :
alk. paper)
　1. Christianity and other religions. 2. Catholic
Church—Relations.
I. Title. II. Series: Catholic studies series.
BR127 .T43 2004
261.2—dc22

　　　　　　　　　　　　　　　　　　　　　2003023940

Printed in the United States of America

♾™ The paper used in this publication meets the minimum requirements of
American National Standard for Information Sciences—Permanence of Paper for
Printed Library Materials, ANSI/NISO Z39.48-1992.

CONTENTS

PART IV: THE HISTORICAL HORIZON OF THE DIALOGUE'S POSSIBLE FUTURE

ACKNOWLEDGMENTS

So many persons, organizations, and communities have inspired this volume. I want to remember in a special way Thomas Keating and his Snowmass Conference; the members of Saccidananda Ashram, or Shantivanam, as it is called, Bede Griffiths's monastic outpost in South India; Pascaline Coff and Osage Monastery; the Bede Griffiths International Trust; the Pontifical Council for Interreligious Dialogue; the Secretariat for Ecumenical and Interreligious Affairs of the United States Conference of Catholic Bishops; the National Association of Diocesan Ecumenical Officers; Monastic Interreligious Dialogue; the Parliament of the World's Religions; the United Religions Initiative; the Temple of Understanding; the World Conference on Religion and Peace; the Fellowship of Reconciliation; the World Congress of Faiths; the Interreligious Engagement Project; the Interfaith Youth Core and the Interspiritual Dialogue Association at the United Nations; UNESCO; the Office on Interreligious Relations and Dialogue of the World Council of Churches; Raimon Panikkar; Diana Eck; Leonard Swidler; and Ewert Cousins, to mention some of the individuals, organizations, and communities that have contributed in a visionary way to advance the value and work of interfaith encounter, communication, and cooperation.

Part I

BACKGROUND

1

THE CONVERSATION BEGINS

The present climate of the world is one of increasing polarization and fear. There is the obvious polarization and, indeed, clash of civilizations currently between Islam and modernity, particularly with Western secularized democracies whose cultures will not tolerate a totalitarian Islamic state in which democracy subserves theocracy and minorities live at the whim of the majority, subject to the Shari'a, or Islamic law, and the often-autocratic rule of the mullahs, who are insensitive to the rights of these minority populations.

There is the division between the haves and the have-nots, the ever-widening gap between the wealthy industrialized societies, under corporate capitalism, and the poorer developing countries that struggle to service their large indebtedness to the Western democracies and the oppressive monetary policies of the World Bank, the International Monetary Fund, and other financial institutions. The victims of this system include more than a billion homeless people around the planet, notably in Asia, Africa, and Latin America, though the tragedy of homelessness also exists in Europe, North America, Japan, and Australia, as one discovers simply by walking down streets in any of the cities in these countries.

There are also the obvious divisions between developed and developing countries relating to education, health care, and economic possibilities. The paucity of opportunities in these areas in the developing nations, where AIDS and illiteracy run rampant, are not made much better by the wealthier nations, which provide minimal assistance and guidance. For example, developed nations are not providing medications for HIV and AIDS in quantities sufficient for the pandemic on the African continent, and so the crisis deepens and widens around the continent and beyond to other parts of the world, notably in Asia, particularly in China and India.

Consequently, the need for dialogue, genuine in-depth communication, should be evident among the nation-states, economic blocs, and disparate cultures as well as among the great world religions themselves, especially Christianity, Hinduism, Buddhism, Judaism, Islam, Taoism, Jainism, Sikhism, and the important indigenous traditions—the Native American, African tribal, shamanistic cultures, and aboriginal faiths. These traditions have a lot of concerns in common, such as the environment, war and peace, terrorism, disease, hunger, poverty, education, economic development, the rights of women and children, human rights, the use of resources, bioethical questions, and justice. On a practical level, the religions share this common ground, since these issues affect all of them in different degrees. The need for the religions to converse with one another is urgent, growing ever more so in this fast-paced, quickly emerging global culture.

The religions also share a common *heart* in spirituality, which unites them not in a formal sense but in the depths of reality itself. This is the one strength and vital resource they can all draw on, as well as their similar moral principles and ethical guidelines with their own rich cultural expectations, applications, and unique expressions unfolded in their individual histories. This strength provides the inspiration for motivation and the resource for transformation of awareness, character, and behavior. It opens hearts and minds, disposing members of the faith traditions to mutual acceptance and ongoing collaboration. It becomes, both in its local reality and in the planetary context, a means of humanization in that very subtle and sustained sense that arises from inner transformation of the heart, the seat of identity in the will and in the consciousness or understanding of persons. Spirituality is perhaps the most important and urgent resource we have to transform the world—the relations among the religions themselves, the nations, cultures, and all peoples—by allowing ourselves to be changed individually. It is a very relevant focus of interreligious dialogue.

THE NECESSITY FOR DIALOGUE

Dialogue is an indispensable activity for humanity, because it requires us to face issues that divide, or could divide, the human family, with all its potential for violence. Thus, there is a practical reason why dialogue must play an essential role in humankind's future. We see how essential it is in the normal commerce between and among governments, in their diplomatic communications, in the United Nations and other international forums, in its role in labor disputes and other kinds of arbitration.

Dialogue also has a central place in relations among the religions. For centuries, even millennia, the various faith traditions have been cultures of isolation, mutually ignorant of one another's history, culture, beliefs, rituals, their positive contributions to the world, society, and the human community. In those ages, communication was minimal, if at all. There was really no perceived need to communicate. All of that has now changed. With the emergence of globalization and the ease of travel to all parts of the globe, cultural isolation is breaking down, and members of the world's religions are meeting one another everywhere. They encounter one another in global forums—in schools, organizations, the military, airports, theaters, and shopping malls and at work and sporting events. There simply is no escape from diversity any longer. We are finally forced by the conditions of contemporary life to accept otherness in all its manifestations, especially in the sphere of religious diversity. If we wish to negotiate this reality of our life now, then we need the tool and the skill of dialogue, of a focused, sensitive conversation. This is true to a much greater extent when it is a question of officially sanctioned communication between Catholics and members of other traditions, a communication that is spreading and taking root in the self-understanding of the Catholic Church, in which certain of its members are given to lives of facilitating and participating in dialogical activities.

We must examine what is meant by the term *dialogue*. This word suggests an attitude of openness to members of other traditions. It presupposes mutual acceptance. Dialogue is an attitude before it is an activity. That is, it requires a state of willingness and generosity of heart to enter into genuine communication with others different from us in faith commitment.

Dialogue as an active form of communication carries an intention of goodwill and respect mutually operative between the interlocutors and all those who engage in this significant practice. It is usually meant as a substantive act of disclosure, or it has to reach this point somewhere along the line in an ongoing process of dialogical relationship. Dialogue, furthermore, in the commitment to communication, is a choice for a peaceful, intelligent, and meaningful relationship with the other(s).

Dialogical life is never a cover for a hidden agenda but an open, honest conversation. It has no other motivation than that of relating to the other in his or her otherness. Neither of the dialogue partners is trying to convert the other or attempting to undermine the other's faith commitment. There is no desire to harm the other's understanding of faith but only a wish to affirm the other in it, respecting its truth, values, and moral beauty. It is to make ourselves vulnerable to the possibility of being deeply influenced in the process of the extended conversation's unfolding. It involves acceptance of the likelihood of being changed by the depth and authenticity, virtue and affection of the other. On a certain existential level, it is a mutual conversion to each other's depth, to the truth present in each.

The capacity for genuine, substantive, humanly enhancing, and intellectually useful conversations that deepen understanding, create bonds of friendship, and expand collaboration on what is critically pressing for the planet—that is, environmental responsibility, the endless work for peace, the promotion of justice, adequate health care, education, and more housing for the poor—is a precious skill humankind requires in the activity of building together a new universal order that seeks to benefit all beings. Such a global society would be a Civilization of Love,[1] a planetary community with a *heart*, an entire social, political, economic, cultural, and religious/spiritual order motivated by compassion, humanity, love, kindness, and concrete mercy. Interreligious dialogue, interfaith encounter, and practical interspiritual explorations are part of this emerging universal civilization and culture.

THE CONTRIBUTION OF CATHOLICISM

The Catholic Church has provided, and continues to provide, valuable leadership in this increasingly significant area, this skill so vital to the survival of the world. This leadership exists on so many levels where we see this gift modeled in various ways. There is the leadership offered by the pope himself in his official teachings as he exercises his magisterial authority, his operation of dispensing guidance in opening doors to deeper relationships with members of other traditions, notably with the Jews, with Buddhists, Hindus, Muslims, Jains, Sikhs, and the indigenous. There is the valuable leadership and guidance of the Pontifical Council for Interreligious Dialogue reflected in its openness, commitment, welcoming, and publications as well as the opportunities it sponsors for in-depth encounters, with theoretical, theological, and practical reflections.

Then there is the fascinating dimension of intermonastic dialogue, which places emphasis on contemplative experience, methods of prayer, the whole range of issues relating to healthy community life, and service to the world. Finally, there is the ordinary level of interreligious dialogue's influence on members of the Catholic Church, the growing culture of sensitivity, and the willing acceptance of otherness in the diverse forms of faith expressed in the many religions of the world. The focus of this book is thus dialogue in all its richness in the Catholic experience, though the primary emphasis is on the official understanding, but with its exciting resonances in the concrete, especially with those pioneers involved in this the most vital and peacemaking work of our age.

PURPOSE AND GOALS

The chief purpose of this text is to strive for a clear understanding of the nature of interreligious dialogue, how it is conceived and practiced in Catholicism. Between magisterial formulations of its conception by the Vatican and theological subtlety there is often a gap. This gap becomes evident—indeed, obvious—in the existential situation of dialogue in which real Catholics are meeting and befriending real Buddhists, Hindus, Jews, Muslims, Jains, and members of indigenous traditions in situations that celebrate our common humanity and all the problems we share as inhabitants of the Earth. We must all be concerned with this domain of dialogical life, since that is where its value and practical necessity are tested.

This book pursues a number of goals for its readers. It seeks to offer a solid, practical knowledge of the dialogical practice as a resource in interfaith encounter, illustrating how it works and its types. It will communicate the great and enduring value of this precious interreligious activity. It is hoped that this book will then inspire young and old alike to pursue further study, perhaps even a career in interreligious dialogue and interfaith work. It is this skill that humanity most needs to cultivate, passing it on from one generation to the next, allowing it to become an essential part of the global culture, along with other values, such as nonviolence, universal peace, responsibility for the Earth, justice, spirituality, and a Global Ethic.[2]

This book is meant for classroom and group use as well as for individual study. The book can also serve as the basic supporting text for original Catholic Church documents and sources.

STRUCTURE OF THE BOOK

After this chapter in Part I, chapter 2 provides a brief historical discussion that presents what is needed to grasp the meaning of interreligious dialogue in the Catholic tradition. It looks at the Second Vatican Council, in particular in tracing the roots. Chapter 3 places the focus on the nature, value, types, elements, and fruits of interreligious dialogue. It is an attempt to uncover precisely what is going on when we are engaged in this situation of cross-cultural conversation.

Part II concerns differing positions on dialogical experience, with chapter 4 examining the example of Pope John Paul II, his reflection, teaching, and inspiring presence in the sphere of interfaith encounter; it seeks to clarify the pontiff's view of the other religions, relations with them, and the role of dialogue itself. Chapter 5 considers the Catholic Church's vision of interfaith encounter and dialogue expressed in its official teachings found in a number of important documents, stretching from Vatican II to the present.

Part III examines what appear to be serious contradictions in how the Catholic Church regards the relationship between its mission of evangelization and interreligious dialogue. Chapter 6 will examine the three options of the Catholic Church, of Christianity, in regarding and evaluating other religions in the light of the church's nature, identity, and mission. These are exclusivism, inclusivism, and pluralism.

Chapter 7 uncovers a basic contradiction, a paradox, that involves the church's commitment simultaneously to evangelization and openness to dialogue, even eagerness to form and maintain relationships with other faith traditions. These two values seem mutually exclusive. We will explore and reflect deeply on this tension and the issues these two values contain. Then in chapter 8 we move on to consider the more fascinating and stimulating area of in-depth dialogue in the intermonastic sphere and, in this instance, the existential relationship between Christian and Tibetan Buddhist monasticism. This is a very rich and profound dimension of dialogical activity, contributing in a substantial way to the Catholic Church's culture of relationship in depth with other religions. It also delves into views differing from those of the Magisterium and discusses the notion of *interspirituality*, the phenomenon of exploring the mystical or contemplative experience of the other traditions.

Part IV is concerned with future possibilities of interreligious dialogue. Chapter 9 develops a vision of the church as the matrix, a more inclusive notion of its identity in relation to the other traditions that includes all the universal concerns of the human family. Chapter 10, the concluding one, dares to dream of the role the Catholic Church could play as the matrix vis-à-vis the Islamic *ummah*.[3] Finally, an appendix devoted to resources and a bibliography round out the book, making it a serious tool for this study.

2

THE HISTORICAL ROOTS
OF INTERRELIGIOUS DIALOGUE
IN THE CATHOLIC CHURCH

The human, existential basis of dialogical activity is gleaned in the nature of conversation itself. We are creatures of dialogue just as we are naturally habituated to conversation. It is one of the activities for which we long and that defines us as human beings. We seek communication with one another just as naturally as we breathe. Here we will explore the origin of the Catholic Church's outreach to and dialogue with other traditions, its cultivation in the Second Vatican Council, and its development in the pontificates of Paul VI and John Paul II. We will mention some antecedent instances and then move on to the council's teaching and that of recent popes.

PRE–VATICAN II EXPERIENCE

It seems there have always been pockets of dialogue between religions throughout the millennia. This is certainly the case in India, which has always experienced an openness to conversations across faiths, particularly on an informal basis. The Indian culture is hospitable to differences and welcoming of the pursuit of the Divine in an individual sense. Asoka, the Buddhist emperor of the celebrated Maurya Dynasty who ascended to the throne in 269 B.C., was a great promoter of dialogue and accepted the diversity of traditions in his empire. He was regarded as the most enlightened ruler of ancient India. The Indian culture's reputation for being open to other faiths no doubt is owed to Asoka's policies.

Contact may have been made between some of the Desert Fathers in the fourth century and Hindus and Buddhists in the Middle East. Buddhist and Hindu communities were present in the area since a century before the birth of Christ. St. Francis of Assisi developed a friendship with the Sultan of Cairo, and Nicholas of Cusa, a cardinal and an official of the Catholic Church, sought harmony between the Christian and Islamic faiths, publishing his *De Pace Fidei* at the time of the fall of Constantinople in 1453. These are a few indications of the possibility of a more congenial relationship unfolding between the Christian faith and other traditions.

In the seventeenth century lived the Jesuit priest Roberto de Nobili (1861–1907), a Roman, who had been sent to the subcontinent as a missionary. De Nobili learned Sanskrit and Tamil, was the first non-Hindu to read the Upanishads, and wrote original works in Sanskrit and Tamil. He awakened to the spiritual authenticity of the Hindu tradition through contact with Hindus, especially Brahmins, and a profound study of their sacred texts. He was especially impressed with their monastic tradition of renunciation, which is called *sannyasa*, and he conceived a new approach that was an early attempt at adaptation—that is, of adjusting the Christian mystery/experience to the Hindu culture.[1] De Nobili was the first Christian to assume sannyasa, discerning an equivalence between his Jesuit religious life and the observance of the Hindu renunciant.[2] De Nobili's relationship with Brahmin pundits, or scholars, and his in-depth dialogues with them represent a significant chapter in Catholic-Hindu encounter.

Similar developments occurred in China with the Jesuit Mateo Ricci and in Japan with Francis Xavier. These men proved to be equally visionary as their brother in the Society of Jesus in India, and all those who followed in de Nobili's footsteps. India, China, and Japan witnessed a creative, imaginative policy of early inculturation, or translation of the Christian experience into the cultural forms, symbols, and gestures of these venerable cultures.

History clearly demonstrates just how far-sighted many Jesuits actually were, and had Rome always listened to the wisdom of these extraordinary pioneers, the Church would have made greater progress in these ancient nations and their time-honored traditions. The Jesuits discovered early on that these cultures were on to a profound spiritual wisdom, and they came to develop a genuine respect for these peoples. The Jesuits proved to be way ahead of their times, but often their recommendations were resisted either in Rome or by some officials of the local church. For example, though he received papal support, de Nobili failed to win over some of the more conservative members of the hierarchy in the Indian church of his time, who were mostly Portuguese. They subverted his experiment at every turn.

Other figures arose in India to advance the Hindu-Christian, or specifically Catholic-Hindu, dialogue and encounter in the depth of contemplative interiority, or mystical cultivation of inner experience. These figures included Brahmabandhab Upadhyay, Jules Monchanin, Henri Le Saux, and Bede Griffiths. Brahmabandhab Upadhyay (1861–1907)[3] was a Brahmin convert to Catholicism who embraced the commitment of a sannyasi as a Christian. In many ways, Upadhyay personified the convergence of the Hindu and Christian traditions. He had absorbed Vedantic mysticism on a very deep level and related it to Christian contemplative wisdom and faith. Upadhyay showed the way to bringing these two traditions together on the mystical and theological levels. He greatly advanced dialogue in a substantive way and positioned Christianity to develop an Indian Christian theology consonant with the genius of the Hindu tradition.

Jules Monchanin (1895–1957), a French priest, and Henri Le Saux (1910–1973), a French Benedictine monk, joined Father Monchanin in Tamil Nadu, South India, in 1948, and together they founded Shantivanam Ashram in 1950 on the banks of the sacred river Kavery in Tannirpalli, Tamil Nadu. They both took sannyasa as Christians to learn from the wisdom of Hindu contemplative experience and to relate the Christian and Hindu faiths on the ultimate level of realization. Monchanin changed his name to Swami Arubi Ananda, while Le Saux changed his to Abhishiktananda, following the Indian custom when renunciation is embraced.[4] The sannyasi's commitment is to the quest for the Absolute, and so sannyasic monasticism represents the deepest form of dialogue. What they and others have achieved since can be called an *existential* convergence, thus bringing dialogue to the highest degree of fulfillment.

Their work was carried on by Bede Griffiths (1906–1973),[5] an English Benedictine monk, who went to India in 1955 to live the Western monastic ideal in an Indian context to dialogue with the Indian tradition of contemplation and relate the two traditions in contemplative interiority. Monchanin died in 1957, and Abhishiktananda left Shantivanam seeking greater solitude in his hermitage of Uttakashi in the Himalayas, turning the ashram over to Bede, who became its spiritual teacher in 1968 until his death in 1973. Shantivanam Ashram had been established to seek the reconciliation of the Hindu and Christian traditions, and Father Bede spent his life pursuing this work. All of these important figures greatly defined the path of mystical dialogue.

THE OFFICIAL OPENING TO DIALOGUE: VATICAN II

Although the Second Vatican Council (1962–1965) never offered a theology of religions, it did explicitly inaugurate this age of interreligious dialogue we are in by changing the Catholic Church's relationship with the non-Christian religions. This change was expressed in a positive perception of the other traditions, in the acknowledgment of the common ground in our origin and end God, in an ontological community and unity of humankind in its supernatural Source.[6]

Nostra Aetate (Declaration on the Relationship of the Church to Non-Christian Religions) is the briefest of the conciliar decrees of Vatican II—barely nine pages—but in light of its historical importance in signaling to the Catholic Church and the world a radically new course and in ushering in a new relationship with the non-Christian faiths, it will ultimately be regarded as having epochal significance. While proclaiming the faith of the church, of Christianity in Christ, it goes on to declare a new responsibility of Christians beyond the borders of their faith, by asserting, "The Church, therefore, exhorts her sons, that through dialogue and collaboration with the followers of other religions, carried out with prudence and love and in witness to the Christian faith and life, they recognize, preserve and promote the good things, spiritual and moral as well as the socio-cultural values found among these men."[7] We are told in clear terms that we are to "recognize, preserve and promote" the moral, spiritual, and cultural insights of the other traditions. Just prior to this enunciated responsibility and task given to us, the council declares in the same seminal document, "The Catholic Church rejects nothing that is true and holy in these [other] religions. She regards with sincere reverence those ways of conduct and of life, those precepts and teachings which, though differing in many aspects from the ones she holds and sets forth, nonetheless often reflect a ray of that Truth which enlightens all men."[8]

This statement is extraordinarily revolutionary for a number of reasons. It acknowledges for the first time in history that truth exists in the other religions, though the Catholic Church had known this about Judaism, particularly in the biblical tradition. It expresses respect for these truths found in the religions, their moral or ethical precepts and other teachings, and, of course, these venerable faiths themselves. This statement and the document as such are also important because of its warm, friendly, welcoming tone and the establishment of a new policy toward the non-Christian religions. It reaches out affectionately to these other traditions, seeking friendship or at least reconciliation. Essentially, however, this powerful statement, and the declaration as a whole, marks the birth of dialogue as a serious, precious value and pursuit of Catholicism, a formulated aim of the postconciliar church.

It should be noted, moreover, that although this ecclesial document concerns the church's new polic—new as of 1965—in relating to all the non-Christian religions, it gives most of its attention to relations with the Jews.[9] Again, *Nostra Aetate* is not really a theology of religions—that must await further reflection and discussion of theologians—but the articulation of a new attitude of the church, and a new intention, toward non-Christians, with special emphasis on the Jews. This course, with respect to the Jewish people, was a well-chosen one, deeply thought out, and embraced.

Part of the reason for this focus of attention has everything to do with the special relationship the church has with the Jewish people in terms of revelation and history. Not only has the Christian faith a relationship of biblical dependence on the Jews, but Jesus was a Jew, as were all of his first disciples and apostles. Moreover, the church's estimation of the Jewish people is also an expression of the deeply felt concern the Catholic Church has for them after the horrendous brutalization and incomprehensible tragedy of the Holocaust.[10]

The Catholic Church, and Christians generally, have recognized a certain responsibility for this historical situation, because of the blatant prejudicial attitudes toward Jews fostered by church authorities for nearly two millennia, culminating in the Holocaust, the historical momentum toward which was generated by the shadow side of Christianity. Christianity did not intend the Holocaust, but its hatred of the Jews, by many of its members, provided the psychological energy and motivation for anti-Semitism.

Vatican II has had an enormous impact on the growth and development of interreligious dialogue and the flowering of the interfaith movement. Without this historical council and its acts, its spirit of openness, acceptance, and respect for all the religions, the interfaith movement might not have advanced at all, and we would still be at square one. It is no exaggeration to say that the interfaith phenomenon owes a huge debt to the Catholic Church. It should also be remarked that many of the leaders in interreligious dialogue come from the Catholic tradition.

This represented a major shift for the church, this change of attitude toward the other faith traditions. It required immense courage in the face of the great unknown. Relations with other religions, the new challenges that the changed attitude would introduce, thrust the church on a course that in many respects is beyond its control. This change of direction demonstrated considerable imagination, inspiration, and trust, but it wasn't enough simply to promulgate a new policy. The church authority also had to create an organization or department to oversee its implementation and the careful regulation of these sensitive relations with the other religions.

In an insightful article summarizing his major presentation to the 1993 Parliament of the World's Religions, the Vatican's representative to this historic event in Chicago echoed the seriousness of the church's decision to go forward with a more positive relationship to the other religions by establishing a special department in the Vatican curia.[11] Pope Paul VI formally created the Secretariat for Non-Christians in his Apostolic Letter *Progrediente Concilio* of 1965. The mission and aims of this agency are set forth in a further document in 1967, an Apostolic Constitution called *Regimini Ecclesiae.*

Later in a reorganization of this curial office in 1984, the name was changed to the Pontifical Council for Interreligious Dialogue. This change was not cosmetic but really quite substantial, and it implemented a fundamental commitment of the Catholic Church to interreligious dialogue itself, and not simply cordial, polite, diplomatic relations with the other traditions. Perhaps this profound change was not envisioned during the council itself, suggesting that the church's understanding of its relationship with the other traditions is evolving, adapting to new moments of insight and historical conditions that surface over the course of time.

The Pontifical Council for Interreligious Dialogue (PCID) has many functions. It carries on the official relations the church has with the non-Christian traditions, while another curial department, the Pontifical Council for Promoting Christian Unity and Religious Relations with the Jews, has responsibility for relations with other Christian churches and with Jews. Everything encompassing the other religions is part of the competency of the PCID. In this capacity, it arranges for formal contacts between religious and spiritual leaders of other traditions and the pope or other church leaders. It organizes events of an interreligious nature that the pope sponsors—for example, Assisi I (October 1986) and Assisi II (January 2002), when Pope John Paul II invited a number of spiritual leaders from all the traditions, including sister churches, to Assisi, the home of St. Francis, to pray for peace in the world and harmony among the religions, nations, and cultures.[12]

The PCID arranges various opportunities for interreligious encounters, dialogues, consultations, symposia, workshops, lectures, conferences, study weeks, and regional events around the globe. It publishes official statements of the pope, the Magisterium, and clarifying documents, papers, and the like. It also has its own journal, the *Bulletin*, or *Pro Dialoge,* which shares important news, upcoming events, and reviews.

POPE PAUL VI'S TEACHING
ON INTERRELIGIOUS DIALOGUE

Paul VI was a very warm and open pontiff, like his saintly predecessor, Pope John XXIII. It was he, following John, who approved the change in direction vis-à-vis the other traditions and placed the church firmly on the path of dialogue. His primary teaching in this crucial area of interfaith relations is enshrined in his great encyclical of August 6, 1964, *Ecclesiam Suam*, which Archbishop Gioia calls "the Magna Carta of dialogue."[13] *Nostra Aetate* was promulgated more than a year after *Ecclesiam Suam.*

The reason for this lofty assessment of the encyclical's historical significance becomes clear upon reading and analysis, since it sets forth the nature, scope, characteristics, and purpose of interreligious conversation in general in the Catholic tradition. It does so from the standpoint, in this instance, of the papal Magisterium, or the teaching authority of the pope himself, which binds his successors to his lead. Encyclicals are highly authoritative teaching documents, vehicles defining direction, policy, and occasions for theological formulation, clarification, and perhaps necessary nuancing.

Ecclesiam Suam draws a clear distinction between the Christian life and the world, or profane existence. It seeks to focus on the gift of the Gospel as totally unique, precious, and effective for the human family. The Gospel is the key to humanity's ultimate happiness, which comes through God's offer of salvation in the Incarnate Son, Jesus Christ. Paul VI lyrically declares, "The Gospel is light, newness, energy, rebirth; it is salvation."[14] He makes it clear that the Church and Christians are in the world, but not of it.[15] It is in the World that the Good News, the Gospel, must be preached. Communicating the vision of the church involves the use of dialogue as a means to fulfill its mission. The church has a sacred duty, a mission, and a mandate to evangelize the world, to announce the Good News to all nations. Dialogue is essentially a work of charity. Because the church has something of extraordinary importance to say, it must dialogue with the world.[16]

It becomes evident beyond all shadow of doubt that the whole rationale for dialogue, as far as the church is concerned, is to advance the message of salvation, the spread of the Gospel of Christ. Dialogue is thus subordinated to and an instrument of evangelization. Dialogue is part of a divine pedagogy the church has adopted to preach the Gospel to all peoples.

Paul VI locates the origin of dialogue and dialogical activity in the relationship between God and humankind, initiated by God himself.[17] This is one of the implications of revelation, or the self-disclosure of the Divine to the human. Dialogue is ultimately about salvation, and Paul VI speaks of the "dialogue of salvation."[18] Love is the motive of this divine initiative, and love should inspire all our attempts at communication with others, especially within this context.

Dialogue, in Paul VI's understanding—and we can say, in the Magisterium's view—is not concerned with the other's point of view as such, though it is taken into account, but with the necessity of sharing the Christian message with interlocutors. It is thus not a two-way street. It has a very practical purpose. *Ecclesiam Suam* puts it as follows: "The dialogue is . . . a method of accomplishing the apostolic mission; it is an example of the art of spiritual communication."[19] Dialogical activity, in this view, is not entered into simply for the sake of mutual understanding, though it certainly doesn't exclude it. Its purpose is to facilitate the preaching of the Gospel. Respecting the freedom and dignity of those who are its recipients, it nevertheless seeks to persuade them of the truth of Christianity, which is why it is said to be "an example of the art of spiritual communication," for it has only a supernatural goal in mind, not a worldly, profane, or secular one concerned with the goods of this life.

Paul VI goes on to identify four characteristics of the church's practice of dialogue: clarity, meekness, trust, and prudence. Dialogical activity has to be intelligible to the hearers of the Good News that the Gospel articulates; it has to be comprehensible and thus have real clarity. Dialogue also follows and expresses a profound humility, a meekness of being. It doesn't arrogantly comport or express itself. In this, Christ is the example, the one who is "meek and humble of heart" (Matthew 11:29). As Paul VI says, "the dialogue is not proud, it is not bitter, it is not offensive. Its authority is intrinsic to the truth it explains, to the charity it communicates, to the example it proposes; it is not command, it is not imposition. It is peaceful; it avoids violent methods; it is patient; it is generous."[20]

Clarity and meekness invite trust from the interlocutor, and this trust often flowers into friendship. Prudence is the fourth characteristic of dialogue, and it is basically a pedagogical sensitivity to the other. It seeks to know the other(s), his or her sensitivities, and to adjust the form of communication to the culture in which Christians find themselves.[21] This kind of sensitivity is becoming more and more the case in our time.

Paul VI warns that dialogue must avoid relativism, and any attempt to water down the faith to get along with those beyond the faith, to bury differences so that we can know a measure of peace and affection in these situations, is firmly discouraged. Dialogue requires a listening heart, an openness of being. He says so eloquently: "The spirit of dialogue is friendship, and even more, is service."[22]

It is clear that what Paul VI means by interreligious dialogue—as does even John Paul II, who builds on his predecessor, as we shall see—is vastly different from what the term *dialogue* means in the interfaith movement itself and in the writings of numerous theologians, such as Paul Knitter, Aloysius Pieris, Raimon Panikkar, and Ewert Cousins, to name a few, where the word connotes a more pluralistic meaning and an openness to hear the other, discussing all the issues that affect us so deeply as human beings. These writers, and so many others (including this one), do not limit the understanding of dialogue to signify opportunities for evangelization of the other partner(s), nor do they subordinate dialogue to such a narrow goal. To do so is to view the activity of dialogue as very one-sided, too narrowly conceived, and very much determined by a theological conception defined by the faith of the Christian vision that squeezes out the other partner in the conversation, who feels perhaps that he or she is not being honored or heard in the integrity of their otherness and the authenticity of their faith commitment. They often feel used and manipulated.

Francis Gioia, following the position on dialogue developed by Vatican II and Paul VI, especially the former's articulation in *Nostra Aetate*, observes that "the sincere acknowledgment of the aspects of truth and goodness present in all religions constitutes a solid foundation for dialogue."[23] From the vantage of the Catholic Church, this statement seems generous and open, but it would be regarded as condescending and one-sided, even cynical, from the perspective of the other traditions who must assume the role of partners in conversation with Catholic interlocutors. Of course it does provide the Catholic side with content for conversation, a place to begin, and I feel this is what can be said in general terms: it is a staring point to begin dialogue, but I doubt it would sustain interreligious dialogue as it develops given the existential situations of persons in such an intimate encounter as dialogue can facilitate.

Dialogue has a way of changing us by altering our perceptions of the other. This activity has a way of making us vulnerable to one another if we enter conversation authentically—that is, if we are genuinely open to the other and willing to learn, and we do not simply impose our view. The dialogical moment and process offer is an equality of opportunity and an existential accountability to the other, as well as to the truth. There is a weight to these factors; they play a substantial role, and they make the classic Catholic theological formulation of Paul VI, Vatican II, and John Paul II difficult to practice in the reality of the existential moment.

In the situation of conversation itself, particularly as the participants become close in friendship as they get to know one another, a sense of accountability to one another, and to the truth, develops. There is a desire not to take advantage, or manipulate the other, or fall into a pattern of merely talking at the other, as we find happens with street evangelists, who show a complete lack of sensitivity to persons of other faiths; they are not open to real dialogue. They are not interested in having an honest discussion but only to preach at the other. The possibility of dialogue doesn't exist in such a context.

POPE JOHN PAUL II'S TEACHING

Since chapter 4 will focus on John Paul's leadership and teaching on interreligious dialogue, this section will be brief. John Paul II's views on dialogue are consonant and in continuity with the guidance provided by Vatican II and the theological direction traversed by his predecessors, particularly that of Paul VI. There can be no doubt or ambiguity in John Paul's clear position on the place of dialogue in the church and his own enthusiasm for it. This pontiff has been eloquent in his support and encouragement of this necessary activity, necessary to the well-being of the world, the other religions, and the Catholic Church itself.

Following the inspiring example of Paul VI, John Paul II has been equally inspiring in his actions and words. He has spoken on numerous occasions during the course of his long pontificate on the importance and need for a dialogical relationship with the non-Christian faiths. In a historic pastoral visit to the Indian Church on the subcontinent in February 1986, the pope characterized his attitude as "a sincere interest in all the religions of India, an interest marked by *genuine respect*, by *atten-*

tion to what we have in *common*, by a desire to promote interreligious dialogue and fruitful *collaboration* between people of different faiths."[24]

This pope has made many statements consistently and persistently calling for interreligious dialogue. For instance, on September 9, 1987, in an address to Christian and Buddhist monks, the pope gave forceful expression of his support for dialogue of the profoundest kind, that which leads to spiritual communion:

> I believe that initiatives which are carried out in this spirit should be promoted and fostered, since we come to know each other better as we humbly tread the path of truth and universal love. . . . Your specific contribution to these initiatives consists not only in maintaining an explicit dialogue, but also in promoting a deep spiritual encounter. . . . May all of you—partners in interreligious dialogue—be encouraged and sustained by the knowledge that your endeavors are supported by the Catholic Church and appreciated by her as significant for strengthening the bonds which unite all people who honestly search for the truth.[25]

John Paul II's enthusiasm is tempered by the limits imposed by Paul VI and Vatican II itself, which have defined the parameters of dialogue, always seen in relationship to the church's mission to spread the Good News, the Gospel of Jesus Christ. We will consider this point in some detail when we come to chapter 4. I want to conclude this chapter with a brief reflection on the practical experience of dialogue, what often happens to persons engaged in it, especially when they become friends.

DIALOGUE IN PRACTICE

When dialogue is predicated on mutual trust and respect, a natural vulnerability develops between and among the participants. Their common humanity becomes a definitive consideration in the nature, extent, and process unfolded in the dialogical development. It is not insignificant but actually quite essential to the success, ultimate outcomes, and fruits of this vital activity. Religious and spiritual leaders, heads of state, foreign ministers, diplomats, and academic and monastic interlocutors have all attested to the richness and depth of encounter when trust and respect are present, and a willingness to be mutually vulnerable emerges in the relationship. The personal relationships that develop are precious, and after a while, they become the point of the whole matter.

Dialogical activity, as a human interaction, becomes an opportunity for the growth of the participants. Slowly, and in its own way, dialogue is changing the world by changing old antagonisms into new possibilities for communion and cross-cultural community. I have seen the miracle of community happen in various situations of encounter from bilateral dialogues between Christians and Hindus, Buddhists and Catholics, Jews and Muslims; in the interfaith movement itself, especially in the Parliament of the World's Religions and the United Religions Organization; or in less formal, spontaneous conversations that just happen between people from different faiths. In the Parliament of the World's Religions, for example, some fifty religious traditions are represented, and I have watched the members of the board of directors coalesce over the years into a working community of people bound together by friendship and an ideal of interreligious solidarity. What becomes clear very quickly when one encounters the Parliament as a living social organism is that it is something radically new: a culture of diversity growing ever more deeply into a harmony of effort, hope, and action for a planetary future that unites humankind rather than ends in greater division, tribalism, and tragic conflicts.

When I attend a Parliament event, like a board meeting, I will look around the table at the fifty to sixty trustees from so many traditions, and I am moved by the affection in which the members hold one another. That feeling is one of the fruits of interfaith encounter and interreligious dialogue. It is accomplishing nothing less than a transformation of old, alienated relationships of cultures to one another. A new humanity is being born that includes all the richness of human experience, belief, and spiritual wisdom.

I marvel and smile to myself when I am engaged in a conversation with Buddhists, Hindus, Jews, or Muslims, to name a few, because we have transcended the need to be right and are enjoying the gift of being related to one another in such a powerful, meaningful way. A wonderful instance of this kind of relationship is seen in a typical dialogue with Tenzin Choegyal, the Nnari Rinpoche, the younger brother of the Dalai Lama. Tenzin Choegyal, or T.C., as his friends call him, loves to be in conversation with others, especially Christians. We have known each other for many, many years, and a wonderful friendship has evolved. A similar friendship also exists between the Dalai Lama and myself, and our conversations are deep, warm, substantive, highly conscious, with much laughter and insight.

T.C. and I have engaged in public Christian-Buddhist conversations. These talks have spanned the years and been held in many parts of

North America, while we have had incredible dialogues for hours at a time in India itself from the inception of our friendship in the 1980s. T.C. was educated by Canadian Jesuits in Darjeeling, West Bengal, India. So, he has a sensitivity toward and an affection for Christians and Christianity. He has a fairly profound understanding of the Gospel, but not an adequate grasp of Christian theology and little real knowledge of the contemplative experience in our long and rich tradition.

Over the years we have discussed the reality, nature, and attributes of God and what Christians, Jews, and Muslims mean by the term. I have tried on so many occasions—sometimes to the wee hours of the morning—to awaken him to the insight that God is more than a concept, considerably more than a projection of the human mind. I've attempted to show him that the concept of God has its origin not in wishful thinking, or fear of death, or even myth, but in mystical experience itself, the realization that long before the concept of God existed, people were encountering this reality in their experience, and indeed, this reality was taking the initiative with them in a mystical way, forcefully imposing itself in a dramatic way on their lives. The evidence for this insight is overwhelming and conclusive, the literature is vast, and the number of mystics who attest to it is endless, especially even in our time.

I have discovered with T.C., however, a kind of an impenetrable wall of perspective that makes it difficult for him to grasp what I've been trying to transmit to him for so long now. My attempts usually end in a bit of humor, of joking with him. Typical is this scenario: I tell T.C. that when he dies and goes through the after-death stages mentioned in the *Tibetan Book of the Dead*, and he has been faced with the Clear Light of the Void, and he opens his metaphoric eyes in that clarity of Light, God will be there to greet him, saying, "Peak-a-boo, T.C.!" to which he responds, "Where's Wayne?" Our conversations end in laughter, which comes out of great mutual affection. In the end, the lesson for me is that I cannot and will not change him, or he, me. Our faiths remain intact, but we are open to the depth and truth present in each.

It is true that with other Buddhists who are better educated, especially someone like the Dalai Lama or one of the many Tibetan masters, much more give and take is possible, and progress on the God issue is occurring. I found this to be the case in an in-depth conversation with the Dalai Lama at the Synthesis Dialogues II in Trent, Italy, in June 2001.[26] We had a genuine breakthrough and epiphany in our exploration of God, Godhead, and Paranirvana,[27] or the ultimate level of nirvanic consciousness. Such breakthroughs are also possible with Zen

Buddhists, notably with a figure like Maseo Abe of the Kyoto School, who has an extraordinarily profound grasp of Christian theology and mysticism, as well as a complete formation in Zazen, or meditation practice.

For decades in the twentieth century, very advanced Christian-Hindu dialogues took place in India. These substantive encounters took many forms: symposia, workshops, panels, whole conferences, bilateral lectures, personal conversations, and live-in retreat experiences. The latter were the most profound, reaching ultimate levels of realization in both Hindu and Christian terms in these precious events. Christian theologians, mystics, and philosophers such as John Chetimattam, Raimon Panikkar, Ignatius Hirudayam, Murray and Mary Rogers, Sister Vanadna, Bede Griffiths, and especially Abhishiktananda were prominent in these extremely valuable interreligious events.

In all of these, and in so many other such dialogical opportunities, the differences persist; each participant's faith and essential commitment remain intact, yet what also ensue are an opening to and experience of the living truth and mystical core of the other's tradition, the contemplative, mystical dimension, which is the source of each great faith complexus. For those veterans of interfaith work who arrive at this level of depth, there is often a mutual *conversion* to the truth present in each other's faith and spiritual experience without losing their identity and commitment to their own faith. This happens where there exists an openness, mutual trust, vulnerability, and a willingness to take a risk for truth, and for the sake of humankind. To me, there can be no doubt that interreligious dialogue and interfaith work are inspired by the Holy Spirit. The reason I say this is simply because something truly wonderful happens when this quality of profundity exists. The interlocutors discover a vital connection with one another and an ineffable bond that transcends their differences. I believe the Spirit is calling us more and more in this age and the ages to come to this kind of realization, this necessary level of awareness, for the purpose of building a new human community around the Earth. If this is true, and only history will prove it so in time, interreligious dialogue becomes an indispensable tool to the survival of our planet, beyond the narrow sectarian interests of any one tradition.

3

THE NATURE, TYPES, AND
FRUITS OF DIALOGUE

We bring to every situation our integral humanity, in both its highest attainments and persistent limitations. No matter how formal an encounter is, whether defined by strict parameters and rules or not, the human element always intrudes, and surely that is often to the good. When our humanness in its heights is present in a dialogical event, our deepest longings, realizations, wisdom, insight, and capacities for generosity, openness, love, kindness, compassion, and sensitivity are operative as so many streams to enrich our vital presence to and communication with others. Let me illustrate this with a true story from my own experience.

In April 1988, I was invited to an important Christian-Buddhist monastic encounter,[1] which was held at Archbishop's House, the residence of the late Basil Cardinal Hume, O.S.B., at that time the Catholic patriarch of England. Returning from a long stay in India, I stopped in Britain for a month, and on April 10, the meeting occurred. The conversation was a short one, a mere seventy-five minutes, involving some twenty monastics of the Tibetan Buddhist and Christian traditions.

An English Benedictine abbot opened the gathering with a brief welcoming, followed by a wonderful perspective-generating intervention by the Dalai Lama, lasting about three minutes. He said, profoundly, "We should have our focus on the far horizon of history where we want to lead humanity. This should be the aim of our dialogue today, as far as I can see." A monk of the Benedictine tradition responded, in a formal theological comment, that we must be very precise about the meaning of our terms to be clear and thus avoid unnecessary confusion. His concerns were more academic than spiritual in this first utterance.

I had intuitively grasped the weight, intent, and spirit of the Dalai Lama's remark. I commented from that depth of understanding or, more accurately, from the perspective of his focus as I inwardly grasped it. He was referring to the necessity of our encounter on the more important common ground that unites us; that's where we want to take humankind. I pointed out, in this context, that we needed to meet on a contemplative, even mystical, level, where we are already one. His Holiness responded with the insight that he felt this was ultimately the most meaningful and inspiring place to engage one another in interreligious discourse.

Here is an instance in which our collective spiritual insight, realization, and consciousness propelled our dialogue to a more subtle degree of meaning beyond words, to a place that might have eluded us if we remained simply engaged on an academic platform. There is no doubt the academic context has its contribution to make and is certainly valuable, but with persons of great, wise experience in these encounters, something of immeasurable value can be achieved, as I believe was the case that day in this particularly rich dialogue. What we gained was a deeper understanding of a more ultimate goal communicated through the subtlety of awareness developed through years of spiritual life/practice, study, and reflection, on both sides. Spiritual awareness and attainment facilitate a more ordinary level of communication that builds on the fruits of such awareness, transfiguring the conversation with higher possibilities. This ordinary level of communication is inspired by the fruits of such awareness and attainment.

In the preceding chapter, we looked at the historical background of the Catholic Church's understanding of and aims in interfaith meetings, its purpose immanent in its commitment to the pursuit of this increasingly vital human activity. We had our first glance at the Catholic view of dialogue itself as it relates to the church's mission to proclaim the Gospel. We also saw the problems this narrow view can create. This chapter will examine the nature of interreligious dialogue, its precious value, its various types, its fascinating elements, and its compelling fruits, or positive effects.

THE NATURE AND REALITY
OF INTERRELIGIOUS DIALOGUE

All human communication has its basis in the social nature of the human person. We are quite naturally given to conversation, in all its forms, especially discussions; affable exchanges between and among friends; debates; arguments; and detailed analysis of persons in government, business, the academy, students, writers, thinkers of all stripes, and just ordinary people living their lives open to the commerce of practical ideas, information, stories, and incidents from daily existence. In all of these situations, and so many others as well, the human propensity to form bonds through verbal discourse and intellectual, creative pursuits finds endless opportunities for expression.

Interreligious dialogue, and all the factors involved in such an exchange, is very much related to this social dimension of human life. It is actually a special case of it and a unique application of the skills of conversation. Interfaith encounter, the opening and reaching out to members of other traditions, is a social act, which carries with it a kind of risk, chiefly the risk of being misunderstood, rejected, trivialized, or simply not taken seriously by those with whom we are dialogically engaged. This social act of communication has the good of the other in mind and does not regard dialogue primarily from one's own perspective. It actively pursues the good of the other and the benefit of all those involved in the conversation. Interreligious meetings of this sort thus require a high degree of preparation, awareness, and the requisite social skills of listening, patience, deep attention, a spirit of compromise, and an attitude of genuine friendliness. All these qualities are interwoven in the personality of the interlocutors, where a measure of sensitivity has developed.

In a very real sense, when we enter into interfaith encounter, we are stepping into a fairly new relationship, an uncharted course whose outcome is unknown. We must take our cue from those who precede us in the journey. Their experience is invaluable and has implications for our own faith, struggles for realization, attempts to live a holy life in the midst of the world and all its pressing cares, its anxieties, that characterize the environment of life in this dangerously divided planet. Pushing out into the uncertainty of the great unknown, we are willing to take risks; explore options; try novel interpretations of our faith in the light of the other's; and make ourselves available to real, necessary change.

Essentially, the nature of interreligious dialogue, what constitutes its very essence, its enduring, definitive character, is the search for and the discovery of our common humanity. It means an adventure into finding, or unfolding the deeper, more subtle reality that always unites us. In this way we get to know one another, from which knowledge springs love, and then onto a depth of abiding communion. It is only in this context, and with this kind of psychoemotional or affective environment, that we can meaningfully discuss our differences—that is, how our faith traditions diverge, as well as how they ultimately converge in a mystical or contemplative kind of direct knowing.

The living reality of dialogue is the fascination and joy of realizing that we are a global family, a universal humankind, a planetary species responsible for the Earth. The substance of interreligious dialogue is nearly always positive, for it usually sheds light on what makes us one, or is the condition for an integral harmony, a human dimension of knowing, being, and acting in all the aspects of our existence as the human race: social, political, economic, religious, cultural, intellectual, spiritual, and environmental, meaning how we treat the Earth and one another in our wholeness or integrity. These are the factors and concerns that unite us, that constitute us all as a single humankind surrounded and sustained by the natural world, the human family that expresses the mystery, glory, and potential of our kind. Dialogue is a journey into perpetual discovery, continual wonder, the sheer joy of amazement in the realization that we are after all the same in the reality of our human nature and all the qualities of being human. This insight is extremely important, pivotal, the starting point, and the end of all our efforts to understand one another. All dialogue, in the context of the meeting of faiths through their representatives, is really about seeking understanding, good relations, and some kind of understanding, with the possibility of authentic friendship.

The nature and often profound reality of interreligious discourse, the heights to which it calls us, the achievements of which it is capable, and the long-term effects it can have of a positive kind between people suggest its precious value. Genuine communication of this type is priceless; its value cannot be estimated, and in this period of history it will be demonstrated to be the very lifeline of civilization, threatened as it is by so much conflict between competing traditions. Anything that advances the cause of peace among the religions must be recommended as having an incalculable place in the scheme of our future history. As long as we continue to converse with one another, engage one another, and work together, dialogue will prove its extraordinary usefulness.

We saw in chapter 2 the narrow view of dialogue proposed by Paul VI and the Magisterium of the Catholic Church. While it is certainly reasonable that dialogue in this context is an occasion to express the truths of the Christian faith, it is not a one-way street. It is also an occasion for the other to present his or her faith in an equal desire to be heard, understood, and respected. Christians in this situation of encounter must be willing to listen to their partners in dialogue as much as they are eager to proclaim their faith.

It must be recognized that competing expectations in the dialogical situation often exist. We've seen the official Catholic expectation, but there are those of the other participants representing both their own traditions and their personal hopes. The personal hopes of the Catholic participants are also present, and these are often determined by their own philosophical, theological, and mystical understanding. Expectations compete in an evolving process of conversation that must take into account the personalities involved, the bonds formed, and mutual impact of views on either side, if it is a bilateral dialogue. As respect and affection develop, expand, and deepen, the personal relationships of the interlocutors will more likely affect the quality, depth, and horizon of the conversations. (By *horizon*, I mean the new possibilities that arise in the midst of the process itself.)

THE VALUE OF INTERRELIGIOUS DIALOGUE

Ultimately, dialogue is a survival skill, and interfaith dialogue may well prove to be the most valuable vehicle for promoting peace and harmony in society and the world between and among members of the religions. This is especially the case when it is a matter of disseminating the seminal value of nonviolence in the interreligious situation. Given the delicateness of this ideal and the state of the world, the only way to properly encourage the growth of this ideal, this crucial insight, this basic attitude, is through the process of dialogue itself. As Martin Luther King Jr. said in his celebrated oration, echoing Gandhi, "The choice is between nonviolence [and] nonexistence!"

In this sense, and in terms of humankind's social, political, economic, psychological, and spiritual evolution, the capacity for dialogue is indeed a very precious acquisition in humankind's continuing development. It represents an advance in consciousness that is basically the emergence and growth of an enlightened activity. It receives its most dramatic scope in the interfaith arena, but the whole accomplishment here applies elsewhere—that is, in all areas of human life. As ideal, value, skill, and eventually an ingrained social-civilizational habit, dialogue is the most forward-looking phenomenon of the third millennium, whose importance becomes more critical with the passage of time and the succession of crises around the world. Although it can certainly be said rightly to have a value in itself, interfaith dialogue is actually in service to all humanity as a species and to the various other dimensions of life on our planet.

THE TYPES OF DIALOGUE

The long experience and practice of interreligious communication reveals a number of standard types or forms of dialogue itself: (1) dialogue of the head, (2) dialogue of the heart, (3) dialogue of life, (4) dialogue of love, and (5) dialogue of the hands. In a mature, well-thought-out process, perhaps all of these types or dimensions will be represented. Certainly in an integral approach, each will have its place, though the dialogue of love must just happen once the intention is set in motion.

The dialogue of the head is the academic level of the conversation and surely is important in the long run if the encounter is not to become confused or superficial. Feeling alone is not enough to sustain such contacts if they are to achieve substance in the communication and the situation of practice itself, the existential reality of the participants facing one another. This can be a very abstract kind of conversation with emphasis on technical and methodological issues involving language and terminology. So many educational organizations are dedicated to fostering these kinds of dialogue and creating ongoing opportunities for exchange. For example, there is the Society for Buddhist-Christian Studies, a number of nonprofits devoted to Catholic-Jewish studies, Hindu-Christian, and Christian-Islamic connections. There is Monastic Interreligious Dialogue, which emphasizes all forms of dialogue, often in relation to texts in the process.

The dialogue of the heart, the second form, naturally engages the affective dimension of human experience. It concerns essentially the reaching out to the Ultimate in spiritual practice, the private activity of spiritual life that is always going on but is shared in a special way during these precious moments of encounter. Whereas the dialogue of the head is appropriately concerned with beliefs, doctrinal differences, abstract principles, and ethics, the dialogue of the heart reaches a depth of experience in shared spiritual practices, such as chanting, singing, meditation, silence, spiritual reading, walking, or a deep kind of meditative listening, all of these out of contemplative practice.

This is the level of dialogue the Dalai Lama referred to as the most fruitful in the narration at the beginning of this chapter. When people of different traditions share common spiritual practices, particularly over a number of days, there's a breakthrough to a kind of intimacy, a contemplative communion that is effective, substantial, inspiring, instructive, and fruitful in the lives of the participants. What is achieved in these deep encounters often makes the work of interfaith encounter and interreligious dialogue so worthwhile, productive, and fruitful in terms of further insights to guide the way forward. Profound bonds develop between participants, and modes of mutual understanding are activated that are frequently not present in more formally academic settings. A real sense of community just happens that pulls the participants closer together in affection and expectation of their common efforts. The dialogue of the heart leaves a permanent effect in their lives, an afterglow that continues to mutually irradiate them, inspiring them on to greater heights of generosity and discovery.

The dialogue of the heart introduces us into the dialogue of life, the third form, which we all share when we are most aware and most alive. It should also be mentioned that the dialogue of the heart is an integral part of this third kind of dialogue. The dialogue of life is an existential realization of participating in the living reality of human nature in some of its finer situations of maturity, depth, and spiritual attainment. It encompasses all that is part of human experience and all those concerns that are closest to everyone: life itself and its transition moments; economic, social, and political well-being; human rights; the search for meaning, direction, and belonging; the reality of suffering; death; and the nature of the afterlife.

The dialogue of life is converse not simply about life itself but existential realization of being together consciously in the process of existence itself. It is an experience of the depth of being, which manifests itself when we relax into a situation of comfort with others in the context of ultimate meaning. The dialogues of heart and life, as well as love and hands, are really about belonging in an ultimate way, something that all the faiths promise but that we have to work at as individuals in our own forms of spiritual discipline.

The dialogue of life is nourished from the one human reality we share because we are the same in that matrix of being. The human condition is the context of this profoundly real conversation that is never without content for the ongoing discussion between and among members of the different traditions, and this point is especially true of the Catholic experience. All of us, regardless of our faith traditions, spring from the same human family, and we are all subject to the same natural law. We have the same needs; know similar joys, hopes, and fears; and all of us suffer, become ill, age, and die. We cry; we laugh; we sing, dance; we create. All our inspiration comes out of the rich soil of life, and so this mystery that surrounds the life we share provides us with a common experience and a common language.

In this shared human condition, with its evolving language, vast streams of wisdom have accumulated over the course of tens of millennia, and these streams nurture our history, our civilization, and especially our religions, which are institutionalizations of those wisdom traditions, concrete embodiments of them in time and space, made serviceable to our many and diverse communities. Out of the reality of humankind's shared occupancy of planet Earth, the conditions of life emerge for all of us. We are all in the same boat. The dialogues of head, heart, and life open us all to the possibility of a practical dialogue of the hands, where we can agree to work together on the critical issues, the conditions we face as the human family in our time, concerns such as war and peace, the environment, homelessness, the widening gap between the wealthy and the poor, universal health care, justice, educational and employment opportunities for all, and many others.

The dialogue of the hands is surely the most urgent because of the world's common problems, and so it is also the most practical dimension of interreligious encounter, one that carries with it considerable promise.[2] This form of dialogue is the fertile area of collaboration on all the concerns of humanity, what faces us all in this dangerous age and in the ages to come. Here, in the beginning of the third millennium, we still face the urgent problem of war, with many conflicts raging simultaneously around the globe. We are confronted with the terrible dangers of terrorism and division, the horrific conflict between the Israelis and the Palestinians, which influences Islamic extremism. All of us, furthermore, live with the blatant disparity between the haves and the have-nots, and the scandalous situation of global homelessness in which more than a sixth of humanity is consigned to the streets and otherwise completely destitute. This situation compels the conscience of each religious tradition and all their members.

The dialogue of the hands urges us to work together assiduously to alleviate this deplorable social evil created by indifference, greed, and neglect. This particular critical issue represents a problem so huge that only an international, interreligious initiative could possibly get a handle on it and move the world toward a solution. When it is considered that more than a billion persons are homeless, it becomes clear that only a monumental effort can reverse this condition, an effort on the magnitude of the civil rights movement of the 1960s, the antiwar activism of the late 1960s and early 1970s, and the opposition to apartheid in South Africa in the 1980s and early 1990s. Everybody knows that the services for these vulnerable people are wholly inadequate, with overcrowded shelters that are often dangerous places where criminal elements and sexual predators oppress the innocent inhabitants, the most exposed being women and children. An interfaith mobilization across the world is the only way to solve this critical matter adequately.[3]

Other interreligious initiatives involving a practical approach to dialogue include the Interfaith Youth Core,[4] founded by Eboo Patel, a Muslim, and Kevin Coval, a Jew, both natives of Chicago and long associated with the Parliament of the World's Religions' youth wing. Both were also leaders at the 1999 Parliament in Cape Town, South Africa. Another organization is called Play for Peace,[5] established in 1997 by Michael Terrien, another Chicagoan; it functions in various parts of the world, especially in India, the Middle East, North America, and Africa, where it brings conflicting communities together through play. It can be noted in passing how this is often a contemplative activity for children in which they transcend their differences in the laughter and joy of the present moment in which they are engaged in a game activity or some other form of playing together. The members of this unique and fascinating organization have actually discovered what can be named the *dialogue of play* itself, which of course is a form of the dialogue of life and, to some extent, of the hands.

A very significant group is the International Committee for the Peace Council[6] that administers the Peace Council itself, an initiative inspired by the Parliament of the World's Religions. It was founded by Daniel Gomez Ibanez, formerly the executive director of the Council for the Parliament of the World's Religions, the organization that directs the Parliament, and a longtime member of its board. Founded in 1994, the Peace Council seeks to advance peace in many areas of the world. It is composed of members or peace counselors from all the traditions, usually spiritual leaders and activists. Besides these are so many other interfaith organizations involved in various dialogical activities, notably projects involving the conversation of the hands.[7]

A very unusual and important Catholic-Buddhist project or an initiative taken that was the fruit of long collaboration between Christian monastics and His Holiness the Dalai Lama is the *Universal Declaration on Nonviolence*.[8] In January 1989, while the Iran-Iraq war was still raging, the Dalai Lama agreed to take a step for peace with Monastic Interreligious Dialogue[9] in the form of a brief document, which constituted a sort of declaration of independence between religion and war making. The prescience of this document becomes so evident in the light of our times in which the clash of civilizations is potentially a conflict between religions.

The need for such a commitment on the part of the religions has never been greater. To promote this insight in the interfaith sphere requires the tireless labor of the dialogue of the hands, the day-to-day nitty-gritty struggle to open hearts and minds through a habit of mutual trust founded on practical collaborations for peace, environmental responsibility, and justice. Interreligious dialogue of a practical nature emphasizing these common concerns can be enormously effective for the planet. They build a habit of cooperation around mutual insights into these common issues, resulting in a consensus and meaningful action.

Sometimes the dialogue of the hands is on a more ordinary level, but no less effective. Bede Griffiths developed such an approach in his community of Shantivanam in South India.[10] Here is a Christian monastic community in the Camaldolese Benedictine tradition that is Hindu in culture but Christian in faith. It is a small Christian center surrounded by a vast Hindu population, and this community is in total harmony with it, relating to the needs of the poorest of the poor in a number of nearby villages and towns. The ashram, under Bede's direction, invested 90 percent of its money into programs to improve the economic lot of the local people by establishing village industries that are owned and operated by the locals, most of whom are Hindus. This is an indication of how concrete the hands on dialogue can be and often is.

Another example is the Tibetan Nuns Project, which is administered by Rinchen Khando, the sister-in-law of the Dalai Lama and formerly the minister of education in the Tibetan government-in-exile in Dharamsala, Himachal Pradesh, India.[11] The whole thrust of this project is to generate the resources to educate Tibetan nuns so that their development is on a par with the monks, who for centuries had the exclusive hold on all educational opportunities. This situation is now in process of change as monastic reform includes extending equal opportunities to women.

Monastic Interreligious Dialogue (MID) has supported the nuns' project from its inception in the late 1980s and has succeeded in attracting the financial aid of individuals, groups, and organizations around North America and elsewhere. Now, many are supporting this worthwhile and needed initiative, the fruit of a long-practical dialogue. There are literally hundreds of such examples, perhaps even thousands, where persons of different traditions are working together in their spheres to improve the lives of others, bring peace to the world, and promote justice in an ecologically sound natural environment.

Oftentimes the most inspiring and effective interreligious encounters happen in far less formal settings, and the most far-reaching transformations occur without even intending them. Let me offer an example from a situation of the dialogue of life. The following happened in my former community of Hundred Acres Monastery[12] in New Boston, New Hampshire, in 1989. The community, under the leadership of the saintly founder, Father Paul Fitzgerald, invited five Afghani mujahideen freedom fighters who had been part of the struggle with the former Soviet Union to live for six months at Hundred Acres. Father Paul had been contacted by the State Department about giving hospitality to them, after they had received medical treatment for their wounds sustained in the war.

When they arrived to the community, only one could speak English. They were from a very conservative Sunni Muslim background, having had little contact with Christians of any sort. All were very warmly welcomed into the heart of the community and were quickly integrated into the natural rhythm of communal life and activities. They ate, prayed, worked, and recreated with the regular membership. No distinction was made between these six and the other twelve members. In this natural dialogue of life, the defenses came down, and they became one of us; they even attended the daily evening mass. A deep affection developed, and these wonderful Afghanis came away from their time with us having had a very positive, valuable experience of Christians.

In my understanding of existential dialogue, the live-in situation affords opportunities for mutual growth absent from the more academic level of dialogue, or the dialogue of the head. Although we need all the types of dialogical activity, clearly there is an urgency, and hence a primacy, to the dialogue of the hands within the context of the dialogue of life. This urgency is evident given the dangerous political and economic tensions that exist today and the fragility of our age when the Earth is threatened by human irresponsibility.

Finally, under various categories of dialogue, we can mention the dialogue of friendship or love. This is a very advanced stage of interreligious relationship, and it is a phenomenon, a reality, I have directly observed many times in a number of formats and contexts. It certainly characterizes my own experience with those of whom I am engaged in interreligious conversation.

The possibility of a dialogue of friendship was brought home to me in the mid-1980s in Madras, South India, when I was fortunate enough to witness some dialogue sessions between Hindus and Catholics at Aikiya Alayam, an inculturation[13] center, founded by the Jesuit spiritual master and theologian, Father Ignatius Hirudayam. Father Ignatius was an expert in Saiva Siddhanta, a southern form of Shaivaism, a Hindu denomination. He was also a consummate master of dialogue, and his love for his interlocutors was always present.

A dialogue of friendship—or a dialogue characterized by friendship, or genuine affection, mutual respect, and trust—is, I believe, the horizon and boundary of interfaith communication. It becomes the container, atmosphere, and substance of communication, the realization that there is a moral and spiritual content to interreligious encounter as in all authentic human interactions. What I witnessed in Ignatius Hirudayam's Hindu-Christian dialogues was a high quality of communion between and among the participants, a living communion of hearts and minds based on friendship and warmth that had evolved through many years of conversation and togetherness, of sharing meals, contemplative retreats, and pilgrimages.

There was no ego competition, nothing to prove, no long, tedious, convoluted arguments or endless debates over minutiae, but the clarity, intimacy, and dynamic unfolding of insight of old friends in conversation. People were completely relaxed and comfortable being themselves, and something truly miraculous always happened. A fluid communion of dynamic insight would emerge quite spontaneously in which a gentle give and take allowed everyone to contribute to the flow of the concatenating vision in a building, cascading effect of deeper and deeper understanding as the communion grew profounder, the insight more subtle in its dynamism and momentum toward a unifying, comprehensive group articulating the theme of the particular topic of discourse. It was the product of a marriage between heart and intellect.

I believe that this quality and depth are only possible where the precious value of friendship animates the encounter and the activity, the human, existential dimension, and the conversations that ensue. I've also experienced this same consciousness in dialogues with Tibetan Buddhists, especially with the Dalai Lama, his younger brother, Tenzin Choegyal, and many others.

THE ELEMENTS AND FRUITS OF DIALOGUE

In this final section of this chapter, I want to consider briefly the practical elements of interfaith conversation and then proceed to examine some of their positive fruits. The elements are really concerned with the structure—logistics, if you will—the content and aims of the interreligious conversational situation. There are essentially five elements, though others can certainly be adduced: (1) intention/motivation, (2) focus/object, (3) method, (4) process, and (5) aims.

When referring to the intention or motivation for a dialogical event or process, I mean precisely the inner reason and hope of the encounter itself. That hope, that inner reason(s), has two sides: the two interlocutors in the encounter, be these individuals, teams, or groups. Each comes to the table with a certain aspiration and expectation(s). The purity of their motivation is the point here. Is it to advance mutual understanding of one another's faith or to build the necessary trust through acts of mutual respect and amity? Is the intention open, clear, and noble? Or is it (or they) hidden, obscure, and ulterior?

Second, dialogues have a focus, a defined object of investigation in the conversation, an agenda for discussion, just like most meetings. For instance, in the Buddhist-Christian Monastic Dialogue on September 5, 1993, at the Parliament of the World's Religions in Chicago, the subject, focus, or defined object was "*Shunyata* and *Kenosis*: The Arising of Universal Compassion in the Spiritual Journey."[14] The focus, subject, or object of the discussion was that of emptiness, or what is called *shunyata* in Buddhism, and its relationship to *kenosis* in Christianity, Christ's process of self-emptying in becoming a human person in this world, taking on the human condition, and of how these two realities are further related to our common spiritual life and development.

Third is the consideration of method in the dialogue. Does someone make a point, raise a question, read a text, and others respond? Or, as in the Chicago event, we each spoke for five minutes on an aspect of the focus that attracted us or attempted to relate Buddhist emptiness with the Christian insight on kenosis. Method has to do with the structure and procedure of the event and how it all ties together. Method is about coherence, consistency, and substance or how substance in dialogue gets articulated in terms of the two positions and the common ground that mediates them. For example, both kenosis and shunyata concern the essential metaphysics of each tradition, their substance, while compassion/love/kindness becomes the common ground they share in the context of the spiritual life.

The fourth element of dialogue is the process itself, the existential reality of persons of different traditions traversing conversations together. Each dialogue has its own process, its unique set of internal dynamics, which is, again, an existential phenomenon; that is, it depends on the concrete situation and the actors in the event. The situation to some extent determines the process, since there are always the imponderables, the factors of the actors interacting as persons in the dialogical opportunity itself, following the structure, method, and content of the event, with the public and private intentions contributing their influence.

Finally, every dialogical encounter, however it evolves, has certain aims, desired goals, actively pursued expectations. These are often long-term and perhaps ultimate, such as building a new civilization on the planet that enfranchises everyone. That would be a goal for the distant future, but we can envision it and other aims along the way. More immediate ones include promoting mutual understanding and enduring relationships or friendships. The aims can also include deepening and expanding contacts, cosponsored projects that are service oriented or scholarly or that emphasize spirituality.

The fruits of interfaith dialogue flow forth from the elements; they emerge quite organically, naturally from the process itself. These positive results are (1) friendship and communion, (2) new insights, (3) genuine depth, and (4) ultimately a new consciousness. Of course these results, benefits, or fruits of this fascinating activity presuppose an ongoing process of conversation in which the participants really experience a bonding.

Friendship is often among the most valuable of the beneficial effects that result from open, relaxed, and amiable discussions. When they are ongoing, over a period of years, the dialogue partners have a chance to get to know one another well, and affection often develops. In time, a tangible sense of communion comes to characterize these encounters, as was mentioned earlier in the instance of the dialogues organized and sponsored by Ignatius Hirudayam. I have seen this happen again and again in my own experience with Hindus, Buddhists, Jews, Muslims, Sikhs, Jains, and Native Americans.

It is always true that dialogue occasions new insights as patterns and connections hitherto unsuspected are recognized; options appear; new ways of conceiving doctrines become apparent; and conceptions and implications of one another's positions become clear. Dialogue, when it occurs in an atmosphere of mutual amity and goodwill, nearly always elicits new understanding of each other's tradition and sheds light on their relationship in ways that are not readily evident.

These conversations that have a history normally reach a level of depth, subtlety, and some real sophistication. This subtlety, depth, and sophistication is not only philosophical, theological, and cosmological but also mystical and contemplative. These conversations so understood reach to the Ultimate Reality, and so they become another area of common ground. This quality represents their depth; their subtlety and sophistication can be suggested in the ways each tradition's view of the Ultimate is able to accommodate with the other's when understood mystically or in terms of direct experience/awareness of the Divine, or Ultimate Reality—that is, in contemplative experience/awareness.

Finally, all genuine interreligious dialogue that is substantial, ongoing or evolving, friendly, with a mutual commitment to one another in affection, flowering into communion, a conversation that arrives at depth, subtlety, and some degree of sophistication, usually bears a relationship to a long-term goal that everyone holds in common and is part of our larger work: the evolution of a new consciousness. This new consciousness bears on our shared hope for a universal civilization that has a *heart*, that works for all, and whose core values are compassion, love, kindness, mercy, equality of opportunity, and the resolution of violence, poverty, and the ecological crisis. Such values and practical social/political/economic goals can only be actualized through the dialogical process in which consciousness on a global scale is affected. It is easy to see how ambitious dialogue can be; its prospects, endless; its blessings, far-reaching.

Part II

VIEWS OF DIALOGUE

4

THE PRESENCE AND EXAMPLE
OF POPE JOHN PAUL II

A pope has an enormously important role to play in the world, and his influence extends around the planet; his voice is heard, even when what he has to say is not popular. This particular religious and spiritual leader sets the tone, defines the direction, and guides the Catholic Church through the course of its earthly history. He can steer it back to the past, courageously guide it into the uncertain future, or foster stagnation in the present through a kind of fearful inertia. More than any other figure, the pope can open the Catholic Church to the other religions in a spirit of mutual trust, respect, exploration, and collaboration, or he can fearfully force the church to recoil into a self-imposed isolation in the face of the challenges of diversity, the demands of interreligious communication, and the unknown effects it will wrought in the fabric of the church's self-identity, faith, theology, and spirituality.

From Pope John XXIII through the pontificate of Pope Paul VI, the brief tenure of Pope John Paul I, and during the long pontificate of the current pontiff, Pope John Paul II, an openness to the other religions has been followed. It was really John XXIII who set the stage for the new relationship with the other traditions that was to unfold from Vatican II onward. Pope John was greatly loved by virtually everyone, even non-Catholics. He was the soul of warmth and acceptance. Openness and an attitude of welcoming emanated from his presence and personality, reinforced by his obvious sanctity, his human qualities of humor, comfort with anyone he was with, and lack of ego. It was his humanness that seemed to draw people to him, and it was from these unique capacities that he could respond to the Holy Spirit's inspiration to summon what was to become the Second Vatican Council. His openness and welcome of otherness resulted in the council being similarly open and welcoming of the other churches and religions.

His successor, Paul VI, similarly embodied acceptance of otherness with a warmth, openness, and a generosity of spirit that extended itself to persons from the various traditions who sought contact with the supreme pontiff. Paul VI's teaching is set forth in the conciliar documents, *Nostra Aetate*, *Lumen Gentium*, and *Gaudium et Spes*, and in his encyclicals *Ecclesiam Suam* and *Evangelii Nuntiandi*. We saw in chapter 2 the thrust of this pope's understanding in *Nostra Aetate* and his powerful *Ecclesiam Suam*. These especially, and many other papal statements during his pontificate, have defined the subsequent direction of the succeeding pontificates of John Paul I and John Paul II.

Pope John Paul I barely had time to do or say anything. He is sometimes referred to as the "September Pope," because of the extreme brevity of his pontificate, extending from August 26 to September 28, 1978. His personality was expansive, and he exuded a wonderful warmth, as did Paul VI and John XXIII before him. He had a contagious smile, and this was an indication of what his leadership might have been like. We have only two documents from his pontificate expressing his possible vision of interreligious dialogue. These are his *Urbi et Orbi*, a speech that popes traditionally give upon their election and on each Christmas and Easter, and his talk to members of the World Conference of Religions for Peace, one of the leading interfaith organizations.

In the *Urbi et Orbi* message, John Paul I echoes his desire to follow in Paul VI's footsteps, when he declares, "We wish to pursue with patience but firmness that serene and constructive dialogue that Paul VI had at the base of his plan and program for pastoral action. The principal theme for this was set forth in his great encyclical, *Ecclesiam Suam*—namely, that people, as people, should know one another, even those who do not share our faith. We must always be ready to give witness of the faith that is ours, and the mission that Christ has given to us."[1] Notice his desire to embrace the path of dialogue and the church's mission of proclaiming the Gospel, thus expressing his intention to adhere to the direction set forth by the council and his predecessor.

In his discourse to the members of the World Conference of Religions for Peace, whose name was later changed to the World Conference on Religion and Peace, John Paul I does not present his vision with any precision or specificity or with the clarity of his *Urbi et Orbi* message. But in speaking to members of various world religions, he intimates the value of dialogue for the church and for other traditions in conversation with it. "In order for peace to be achieved, it is necessary that the need for it should be felt profoundly by the mind, as something born from a fundamentally spiritual conception of humanity. This religious aspect encourages not just pardon and reconciliation, but also a commitment to promote friendship and cooperation between individuals and peoples."[2] John Paul I hardly registered a direction at all, but it is significant that he met with members of this interreligious society and expressed the spirit of Paul VI's understanding.

In this chapter, the focus is on Pope John Paul II, who unlike his immediate predecessor has had quite a lot to say about interreligious dialogue and who has been and is an inspiring figure in the Catholic tradition and on the world stage, revealing through his presence, example, attitude, personal views, and official teachings an abiding support for and encouragement of interfaith encounter, dialogue, and close collaboration between the Catholic Church and the other religions. In what follows, we will explore together this pontiff's spirit of dialogue with the non-Christian religions, his personal presence, example, attitude, actions, or initiatives in promoting the church's relations with these other traditions, especially in the fostering of mutual collaborations for peace toward a new civilization with a heart. A sample of his personal views on Buddhism, Islam, and Judaism will also be offered.

JOHN PAUL'S PRESENCE, ATTITUDE, AND EXAMPLE

John Paul II, like his predecessors, has made himself available to the religious and spiritual leaders, writers, and scholars of the various religions throughout his long pontificate. On numerous occasions, in welcoming these persons to the Vatican, even while having meals with some of them, he has told them that they are always welcome here, meaning at the Vatican's Apostolic Palace. Although theologically conservative, this pope is deeply committed to interfaith encounter and dialogue. He has expressed this support on numerous occasions and in many parts of the world, in symbolic gestures such as visiting a mosque, synagogue, or temple; meeting with representatives of other traditions; and offering formal and official teachings of his Magisterium. Some of these we will examine in the following chapter. He has forged bonds of friendship with a number of these leaders, including the Dalai Lama, the Tibetan spiritual and temporal leader.

Some years ago, the Dalai Lama shared with me a few instances of his many encounters with John Paul II. He mentioned to me that he and the pope are friends, and then he detailed the numerous times and situations they had met, what they talked about, and the bond that had developed between them, two persons from completely different cultures, having so much in common, especially their shared suffering, since both came from nations oppressed by communist regimes. Though it is true that the Catholic Church, in its official structure and government, has done nothing tangible for the Tibetan people, John Paul II has expressed support for the Dalai Lama and the Tibetan nation on a symbolic level, especially by receiving His Holiness so many times and in such a friendly way.

This pope has been a wonderful model of acceptance and fraternal love for the Jewish people and has many long-term friendships with Jewish spiritual leaders. He has done so much to free the Catholic Church, and Christianity in general, from its anti–Semitic past; he has healed the relationship with the Jewish people, and established diplomatic relations with Israel. Under his wise leadership, the work of dismantling anti-Jewish cultural currents in the Christian tradition, notably in its theology, has flourished and succeeded, a labor begun during the pontificates of John XXIII and Paul VI. We will discuss this relationship later.

Assisi I and II attest in a dramatic historical way to his firm commitment not simply to dialogue but to genuine collaboration between and among the religions. This commitment to dialogue and cooperation, in practical terms, stems from his recognition of the utter necessity of the religions to seek harmony among themselves and be agents of peacemaking in the world at large by first promoting peaceful relations between and among themselves, extending it then to the nations of the Earth. We will consider the two Assisi events as well.

One of the first substantial statements of this pope's commitment to interreligious dialogue came in an address he gave during an audience to the membership of what was then called the Secretariat for Non–Christians,[3] the department in the Vatican Curia charged with overseeing the church's relations with other religions, established by Pope Paul VI in 1964 during Vatican II. This audience was confined to just the staff of this curial office, and so a certain intimacy of communication was present on this occasion. The audience occurred just six months after his election on October 16, 1978, the audience happening on April 27, 1979. Archbishop Michael Fitzgerald, now the president of the Pontifical Council for Interreligious Dialogue (PCID), in an article entitled "Pope John Paul II and Interreligious Dialogue," reflects on this important audience of the membership of his department with the then new pontiff. He comments that the pope had anticipated the question on everyone's mind: Would he have a commitment to relations with the other religions as Pope Paul VI had?[4] Emphasizing continuity, Fitzgerald reports:

As a reply, John Paul II referred to his first encyclical letter, *Redemptor Hominis*,[5] published the previous month. In that document, he had underscored the way the Second Vatican Council had seen the globe as a map of various religions impinging on the Church's own self-awareness. He spoke of the deep esteem shown in the Council documents for the spiritual values enshrined in other religions. He concluded: "The non-Christian world is indeed constantly before the eyes of the Church and of the Pope. We are truly committed to serve it generously."[6]

It is clear from this instance, as well as from his enthusiastic support through his presence, his example, and his numerous statements and official magisterial teachings, that this pontiff is a champion of interreligious relations and that he regards these relations as very precious to the Catholic Church, as well as to himself personally. His life, particularly during his ministry as supreme pontiff, is an eloquent witness to that incontestable fact.

This pope is clearly aware of his responsibility to be a vehicle of evangelization, of proclaiming the Gospel to the world on every occasion, but equally he is in his own element—indeed, relishes his role as a bridge between and among the great traditions of humanity. The word *pontiff* comes from the Latin word *pontifex*, which has to do with bridge building, as in *potem facio*, to make bridges, or one who cares for the bridges of Rome. One of the titles of the pope—whoever he is—is *Pontifex Maximus*, a high priest, which in the Roman Empire was the equivalent to being the mayor of Rome. More than ever, a pope must be a communicator, one who draws the world together, a builder of bridges not simply within the Christian world but between this tradition and all the others.

The Pontifical Council for Interreligious Dialogue held a plenary assembly in Rome on November 13, 1992, at which John Paul II spoke. In that event, he made it very clear how important dialogue and interfaith relations are to him. Addressing the PCID, he said, "Your work contributes to the fulfillment of what I have always considered a very important part of my ministry: the fostering of more friendly relations with the followers of other religious traditions."[7] In reporting on the participation of the pope in this occasion, Archbishop Fitzgerald remarks that John Paul II has made a very significant contribution to the church's official teaching concerning the place and function of the other traditions in God's design or, as he says, "plan of salvation."[8] As if to underscore the role of the pope today in the context of the meeting of the religions, the archbishop goes on to say, "He [John Paul] shows moreover that he does not consider his role to be confined to the Catholic Church alone."[9]

His record on this score is quite impressive, ranging from his ecumenical activities of reaching out to the Orthodox Church, the Anglicans, and other Reform churches; participation of the Vatican in the World Council of Churches in Geneva by way of an observer representing the pontiff; his cultivation of warm relations with the Jewish community; his support of the World Conference on Religion and Peace, the Parliament of the World's Religions through church representatives either from the Holy See or from local churches, such as London, New York, Chicago, Delhi, and Paris, to mention a few, and other interfaith organizations; his countless encounters with members of other traditions in various parts of the world as well as in Rome; and his numerous statements demonstrating a spirit, tone, and leadership wide open to dialogue and practical collaborations for peace, justice, environmental responsibility, education, health care, and a more equal sharing of the goods of the Earth.

He has met with Buddhist leaders over the years, at the Vatican and in other parts of Europe, Asia, Africa, and North America, just as he has consistently had many exchanges with members of Hinduism, Judaism, Islam, and other traditions. On September 26, 1979, John Paul received in an audience a number of Buddhist monks who had lived in various Catholic monasteries in an intermonastic exchange program. He expressed his enthusiasm for this kind of experiential event in interfaith encounter of the dialogue of heart and life, commenting, "Your experience is truly an epoch-making event in the history of interreligious dialogue."[10] These sentiments and spirit are fairly typical of his outreach to Buddhists and representatives from any other faith tradition.

For example, in remarks to representatives of the Hindu community in Nairobi, Kenya, the pope affectionately recognized Kenyan Hindus and mentioned the joy it gave him to be in their presence in East Africa. He went on to say:

> Your own roots are found in the venerable history of Asia, *for which I have much respect and esteem* [italics mine]. In greeting you I willingly recall the fact that the Second Vatican Council, in its Declaration *Nostra Aetate*, manifested the fraternal attitude of the whole Catholic Church to non-Christian religions. In this she showed her task of fostering unity and love among individuals and nations and her commitment to advance fellowship among all human beings. Special reference in the document was made to Hinduism and to the religious values embraced by its followers. Today the Catholic Church is willingly associated with all her brethren in a dialogue on the mystery of man and the mystery of God.[11]

He is treading a path of continuity with Vatican II and Paul VI; he is completely in accordance with the spirit of opening to the world that John XXIII incarnated in his brief pontificate of 1958–1963.

King Hassan II of Morocco invited John Paul in 1985, the International Year of Youth, to visit his country and address his youth, most of whom were Muslims. This visit occurred in August, and in a substantive talk to a large assemblage of young people, he emphasized the common ground between the Catholic Church and Islam, chief of which is the same God, the Father of us all. In a long discourse to this gathering, he observed the substance of the ground the two traditions share:

> I believe that we, Christians and Muslims, must recognize with joy the religious values that we have in common, and give thanks to God for them. Both of us believe in one God, the only God, who is all justice and all mercy; we believe in the importance of prayer, of fasting, of alms-giving, of repentance and of pardon; we believe that God will be a merciful judge to us at the end of time, and we hope that after the resurrection he will be satisfied with us and we know that we will be satisfied with him.[12]

His intention in this eloquent discourse was to acknowledge and praise the spiritual treasures and depth of Islam, with the hope of inspiring young Muslims, drawing them into an enthusiastic dialogue with the Catholic Church, with the precious substance and depth of the Gospel. By reaching out to these youth in their own terms, showing genuine respect to the integrity of their faith, he was, again, building a bridge between Christianity and Islam through an appeal to the minds and hearts of its idealistic and faithful youth.

This approach and dialogical methodology is evident throughout his years of relating to the representatives of the other traditions. Always he sets the stage for dialogue by being concretely an example of openness and respect, radiating a sincere desire to communicate with others, calling them into the light of that common ground we share.

We see this pattern and methodology at work when he made his celebrated journey to India in early February 1986. In an important speech we can discern his affirming attitude of India's great spiritual culture, and it is clear that he has a profound appreciation of its mystical authenticity, its antiquity, and its enduring universal spiritual values, which are eternal, like those of Christianity. In an address to the religious, spiritual, and cultural leaders of India meeting in Calcutta on February 3, 1986, the pontiff stated:

> In speaking to you, men and women of the academic world, representatives of the world of art and the sciences, religious leaders, I cannot but underline the Catholic Church's esteem for the manifold cultural life which you represent. The Church rejoices at the creative richness which has characterized the culture of India during its history of thousands of years. During this time it has preserved a marvelous continuity and a subtle unity in the midst of a wide variety of manifestations. Its vitality and relevance are borne out by the fact that it has molded many sages and saintly mystics, poets and artists, philosophers and statesmen of great excellence. Yes, the Church looks in admiration upon your contribution to humanity and feels so close to you in so many expressions of your ethics and your asceticism. She attests to her profound respect for the spiritual vision of man that is expressed century after century through your culture and in the education that transmits it.[13]

Here is a statement suffused with the glow of understanding the nature of India, with a profound sense of connection with its spirituality, moral vision, and experience of the unity of life obtained by the trial and error of its philosopher-mystics, contemplative sages, and great spiritual geniuses.

In all of this, however, he is still the pope, head of the Roman Catholic Church, with more than a billion members, or one-sixth of humankind. Although he consistently expresses his and the church's respect for the faith of those to whom he is speaking, he is still addressing them as the leader of the Christian world, a third of the human race! In that same inspiring discourse just quoted, he goes on to refer to the church's arrival to and place in India, and here we have an indication of the other side of dialogue for a leader of the Catholic Church: the overarching value of evangelization.

In the spirit of a subtle kind of evangelism, John Paul II asserts about the Catholic Church on the subcontinent: "She is pleased that, from the beginning, Christianity has become incarnate on Indian soil and in Indian hearts."[14] He never deviates from his mission in all the situations of his pontificate wherever it takes him and to whomever he speaks. He is aware, keenly conscious of his overriding responsibility to the Gospel, to proclaim its truth to all who will listen. Archbishop Fitzgerald points up this duality in the pontiff—that is, on the one hand, his evangelical activities on behalf of the Christian tradition and, on the other, his untiring work to open doors to and establish deeper bonds with all the other religions of the planet. Near the end of his article, he says, "John Paul is looked upon as the leading evangelist of our time. . . . At the same time, no Pope has done as much to foster dialogue with Jews, Muslims, Buddhists, and indeed with people of all religions."[15] He has accomplished more than any other pope in history to advance interfaith understanding through dialogue and collaborative initiatives.

INITIATIVES OF POPE JOHN PAUL II

Earlier we have seen in these instances the example of a deeply committed pontiff to the great opening to the other world's religions inspired by Vatican II, John XXIII, and Paul VI. He has also followed their lead on ecumenism in seeking re-union with the Orthodox Church and the other Christian communions. He hasn't simply followed in his predecessors' footsteps but has broken new ground, taking historic initiatives as in the two Assisi events of October 27, 1986, and January 24, 2002. He has placed great emphasis on the church's relations with the Jewish people and has personally been involved in developing closer ties with the Jewish community around the world. We will examine these initiatives and actions of the pope in this and the following section.

This pope has been vigorously active in seeking closer relations with the Orthodox Church, the Anglican Communion, and other Reform churches. His personal relationship with the Ecumenical Patriarch Bartholomew I, the primate of the Orthodox Church, is very warm, and relations between the Holy See and the Orthodox Church are improving with the passage of time, though relations with the Russian Orthodox are strained.

John Paul II met with Ecumenical Patriarch Bartholomew I in Rome in the latter half of June 1995—one of their many occasions for meeting—and one of the issues of this particular official encounter was interreligious relations as well as ecumenical concerns. They discussed many issues of common interest, especially as these relate to the critical problems of our age: the ecological crisis, the disparity between the haves and have-nots, the need for peace, the work for justice, ecumenical efforts, and the importance of interfaith relations. In a joint declaration dated June 29, 1995, that they both signed, they draw attention to their commitment to dialogue. This declaration represents a very important act on the part of both church leaders. They each understand the need for both ecumenical and interreligious dialogue. In their joint declaration, they proclaim:

> In meeting one another, the Pope of Rome and the Ecumenical Patriarch have prayed for the unity of all Christians. . . . They bear in their heart a concern for all humanity, without discrimination according to race, color, language, ideology or religion. They therefore encourage dialogue, not only among Christian churches, but also with the various religions.[16]

One of the implications of their joint communiqué is that they, and their communions, are allies in the interfaith work but also in the larger project: building a civilization of love, which John Paul II and Paul VI have always had before them as an integral part of their ultimate vision for the human family. (We will have more on this later when we consider Assisi II.) John Paul is well aware that bringing into being a new universal civilization will require the cooperation of the entire world, especially all the faith traditions. The vision of a civilization based on selfless love, or agape, in the Christian understanding, is the fruit of applying the Gospel to humankind's future and the historical dynamics of the evolution of human consciousness.

The pope also has reached out to the World Council of Churches, which has a regular institutional link with the Catholic Church, or the Holy See, through the PCID, and they meet routinely. On one such gathering in Rome with the World Council of Churches' special entity corresponding to the PCID, which is called the Dialogue Section, the pontiff intimates the need to work together: "Certainly, your commitment is not limited solely to what you can accomplish on your own. You are also concerned about what is being done in this field by all Christian groups."[17] Christians should work together in a larger purpose than just the interests of their particular communities. He points out how interreligious dialogue has a lot to do with transforming relationships, and this goes beyond individual awareness—it reach the masses in each tradition. This is the substance of the work certain Christians and members of other traditions are engaged in, as they reach out to our friends in other faiths. He clarifies by being more specific:

> The effort to build respect, understanding and trust at the popular level is a condition for friendly relations among the followers of the

great religions. The vision and the goodwill of individuals alone is not sufficient to affect deeply the relations between communities of believers. The vast numbers of ordinary believers must also come to understand and accept people of other faiths as brothers and sisters with whom they can peacefully share their lives.[18]

We require these visionary individuals in our communities, but their awareness must spread to all believers. The few who have this advanced consciousness are not enough to transform the world. Our communities need to be transformed. The question is, how to extend this awareness to the whole tradition—that is, to the larger membership?

JOHN PAUL II AND HIS RELATIONS WITH THE JEWS

It is no exaggeration to say that no pope has done more to improve relations between the church and the Jewish people than John Paul. We will explore this topic more deeply in the next chapter, but here I want to draw attention to John Paul's personal example and valuable leadership in this area.

There can be no doubt that this pope's Polish background has played a major role in how he has come to regard his own responsibility toward Jews. He witnessed their brutalization in Poland by the Nazis. He saw the terrible anti-Semitism of some of his countrymen. No doubt he came to understand the responsibility Christianity bore in all of this, especially the Catholic Church, for the Holocaust didn't happen in a vacuum. It was preceded by centuries of blatant hostility toward the Jewish people, reinforced by theological opinion that blamed them for the death of Christ and so regarded them as guilty of deicide. The Holocaust is not only essentially incomprehensible and beyond conception, defying any attempt to "domesticate" it for Jews; it equally defies understanding and familiarity for Christians.

John Paul II is a spiritual leader in the Catholic Church who has done his moral homework when it comes to this dark and ugly reality. He has known the anguish of one who must assume the conscience of the Christian people, especially in realizing the depth of moral failure of Christians in relation to Jews. If anything can be named sin, it is definitely how the Jewish community has been treated throughout most of the church's history until fairly recently, at least until the Second Vatican Council. This overpowering and sober realization undoubtedly is always near the surface of the pope's thoughts and must have entered into his statements, actions, and gestures toward healing this vital relationship of the two venerable communities of faith. This process of healing, in all its dimensions, and granting special recognition—indeed, the intimacy of friendship to the Jewish people—is one of the enduring hallmarks of his long and rich pontificate. His words, actions, and symbolic gestures have paved the way to an evolving friendship.

April 13, 1986, was a profoundly momentous day in the history of Jewish-Christian relations; it represented a world historical event. On that day, Pope John Paul II made a long-expected visit to the chief Jewish synagogue in Rome, the most important spiritual center for the Jewish community in Rome, a community that has continuously lived there since the time of the Roman Empire. This papal visit received worldwide attention at the time. The pope's focus of attention, in his speech to the Jewish community, is on the historical significance of the event, bringing the two communities of faith closer together. He reflects:

> I would like, together with you, to give thanks and praise to the Lord . . . because it has been his good pleasure, in the mystery of his Providence, that this evening there should be a meeting in your "Major Temple" between the Jewish community that has been living in this city since the times of the ancient Romans and the Bishop of Rome and universal Pastor of the Catholic Church.[19]

The pope remarks about the actual event and meaning of his encounter with the Jews of Rome. He recalls with fondness the visit of the chief rabbi, Elio Toaff, to the Vatican in February 1981, and he mentions numerous occasions of meeting at the Vatican between world Jewry and officials of the Holy See, including the pope. He harkens back to the pontificate of John XXIII, a much-beloved pontiff, and his wonderful warmth, openness to, and affection for the Jews, especially those in Rome. John Paul mentions that he wants to follow his heritage in relation to the Jews.[20]

He then turns to the Jews' terrible sufferings throughout their history after the Diaspora, particularly during the dark time of the Nazi regime. He clearly expresses how disgusting the earlier manifestations of hatred and discrimination against the Jews were, and he reinforces this moral statement by referring to the guidance of *Nostra Aetate,* "[which] deplores the hatred, persecutions, and displays of anti-Semitism directed against the Jews at any time and by anyone."[21] Then he says with a dramatic soberness of concentration, "I would like once more to express a word of abhorrence for the genocide decreed against the Jewish people during the last war, which led to the holocaust of millions of innocent victims."[22]

The pope then mentions a historic visit he made on June 7, 1979, to the infamous Auschwitz, the horrific concentration camp in which so many died, and he recommends, along with the Jewish people, that the Holocaust always be remembered and reflected upon.[23] He goes on to refer to the suffering of Italian Jews during the Nazi period and how the Catholic Church secretly gave them sanctuary in its various institutions:

> The Jewish community of Rome, too, paid a high price in blood. It was surely a significant gesture that in those dark years of racial persecution the doors of our religious houses, of our churches, of the Roman seminary, of buildings belonging to the Holy See and of Vatican City itself were thrown open to offer refuge and safety to so many Jews of Rome being hunted by their persecutors.[24]

Granting refuge to the Jews of Rome, and Italy more generally, was a decision made directly by one of his predecessors, Pope Pius XII, and influenced by one of his advisers, Mother Pascalina. This was a bright moment in an otherwise terribly dark time, one that was not the best moment in the pontificate of Pius XII or in the moral history of the Catholic Church.

This particular encounter between the pontiff and the Jewish community of Rome can be seen as a turning point in a relationship that has become progressively closer, more intimate between not simply the pope and the Jews, but more broadly between the Jewish people and the Catholic Church. In all of this, John Paul II has played a central role. We will return to relations with the Jewish people and the Catholic tradition in the next chapter as we consider more official teachings and the formal statements in this papal address to the Roman Jews.

ASSISI I AND II

John Paul II's record of statements, teachings, actions, visits, and audiences is quite impressive. He has referred to the importance of relations with non-Christian religions on hundreds of occasions. These remarks have occurred in encyclicals and other papal documents; in letters to church officials; to bishops making their *ad limina*[25] visit; to ambassadors and the whole diplomatic corps accredited to the Holy See; to heads of states and United Nations (UN) officials; to the PCID and other departments of the

Roman curia; to members of religious orders; to gatherings of people of various traditions in every part of the world on his numerous journeys; to the spiritual and religious leaders of the other world's religions, to interfaith organizations, conferences, and special synods;[26] to students, scientists, theologians, philosophers; for the annual International Day of Peace and other occasions; to general audiences and liturgies; to the UN in person and other forums and contexts; as well as frequently to the faithful gathered in St. Peter's Square.

Two events that have great historical significance as initiatives of this Polish pope are the Assisi meetings with the leaders of the various religions and the pope in the tiny city in Umbria, northern Italy, the hometown of St. Francis. These took place on October 27, 1986 (Assisi I), and January 24, 2002 (Assisi II). Both of these gatherings were at the pope's initiative and reflected decisions that he himself had made, and perhaps each was his own idea. John Paul II attaches considerable importance to the Assisi meetings, viewing them as collective actions with other spiritual leaders for peace and as steps toward a Civilization of Love, the great dream of his predecessor, Paul VI. The Assisi process reveals clues to the pope's vision and hope for this new universal order with a heart, and perhaps they indicate John Paul's commitment to interfaith dialogue and the evolution of friendly relations with all the other faith traditions.

ASSISI I

When John Paul invited a number of religious and spiritual leaders together to pray with him in Assisi for world peace, he was aware that this event was historically monumental. Archbishop Fitzgerald observes, "Undoubtedly the most important initiative the Pope has taken in the field of interreligious relations has been the Day of Prayer for Peace held in Assisi."[27] It has had an enormous impact both within the Catholic Church and on its relations with the other religions. The impact on the church itself has been twofold; that is, it has occasioned both praise and controversy. The vast majority of Catholics who have been aware of this rare and unusual occurrence were curious, some elated, and many inspired by it. There was, however, a tragically negative reaction by a tiny group of Traditionalists,[28] led by the dissident French archbishop Marcel Lefebvre, later excommunicated, who reacted with hostility and an open defiance of Rome and papal authority. Lefebvre and his band of conservative rebels interpreted the Assisi event as apostasy by the pope.

Bede Griffiths, the saintly Christian mystic sage in South India, had a completely different reaction. He saw this Assisi encounter in 1986 as an extraordinary turning point in the church's relations with the other world's religions. Certainly, allowing representatives to be seen publicly with the pope on a seemingly equal footing suggests a fundamental change in how they are regarded. This is one of the reasons for the harsh reaction of the Traditionalists.

Assisi I drew some of the most celebrated spiritual leaders, including the Dalai Lama and the archbishop of Canterbury; a number of other central figures were also present—Orthodox bishops, Islamic imams, mullahs, and many Buddhist, Protestant, Jewish, Hindu, Native American, and other indigenous spiritual leaders. As a symbolic event, Assisi I was unparalleled, and this truth was communicated by the presence of such diversity.

In terms of content, it was also extraordinary. The focus was applying the activity of prayer as a resource in peacemaking, of inspiring the nations, cultures, and religions of the world forward to a stable global peace. Fasting was embraced by everyone, as was a spirit of silence. Each group of the participants were assigned a church in Assisi to pray in their particular way. The invited guests of the event did not pray together, but they united their intention for peace with the pope's and with the other religious and spiritual leaders. Assisi I was a spiritual act, an act pointing to the power of faith, but it was also a moral act. The pontiff observed:

> The coming together of so many religious leaders to pray is in itself an invitation today to the world to become aware that there exists another dimension of peace and another way of promoting it which is not a result of negotiations, political compromises or economic bargainings. It is the result of prayer, which in the diversity of religions, expresses a relationship with a supreme power that surpasses our human capacities alone.[29]

This is really an astounding statement of the triumph of the vision of faith, and the power of prayer to transform the world by transforming us, our societies, and the international community through its members. The pope's initiative at Assisi is a unique one, related to his ultimate vision of a Civilization of Love, a vision that can only become an actuality with the collaboration of all the religions and of all conscious, aware persons as fully active, committed participants. In this process, the whole dimension of prayer, in its multiformity, is a vital resource. He is confident, even certain, that every member of the Assisi gathering is dedicated to the welfare of the human family and the peace of the world.[30]

The pope goes on to emphasize pilgrimage, within the context of the sacred places in Assisi associated with its great saints—Francis, Clare, and Leo—and the utter necessity for repentance, conversion of heart, humility, trust in the Divine, and an openness of heart in the depth of a kind of contemplative silence. He tells the gathered spiritual leaders and the watching world that he has chosen Assisi for the World Day of Prayer for Peace because of St. Francis, who is "a symbol of peace, reconciliation and brotherhood."[31] It is, after all, Francis who in his celebrated prayer opens with "Lord, make me an instrument of your peace," and the pontiff recites this Prayer of St. Francis at the conclusion of the day.[32]

ASSISI II

Just as Assisi I was a crucial juncture in the development of Catholicism's relations with all the religions working together with the Catholic Church to transform the world by first working for peace as foundational to the greater collaborations for building a Civilization with a Heart, Assisi II was similarly another important moment in the church's attempt to inspire the religions to work with it for peace and for greater things. The work for peace is the same labor as Assisi I because the challenges to the harmony and well-being of the world are extreme. There is the urgent problem of terrorism, and the religions must be united in their moral struggle against it. On January 24, 2002, the pope alluded to this very disturbing global issue: "We wish to do our part in fending off the dark clouds of terrorism, hatred, armed conflict, which in these last few months have grown particularly ominous on humanity's horizon. . . . The shadows will not be dissipated with weapons, *darkness is dispelled by sending out bright beams of light.* . . . Hatred can only be overcome through love."[33]

Assisi II met in a spirit of hope but of soberness as well, and some fear for the future after the tragic events of September 11, 2001. John Paul drew attention to the responsibility of religion and religious leaders to reject the use of violence and not to encourage it or pass over it in silence when there are graphic instances of it breaking out in the world and reflected in the news.

> It is essential . . . that *religious people and communities should in the clearest and most radical way repudiate violence,* all violence, starting with the violence that seeks to clothe itself in religion, appealing even to the most holy name of God in order to offend man. *To offend against man* is, most certainly, *to offend against God.* There is no religious goal which can possibly justify the use of violence by man against man.[34]

The pontiff and the other spiritual leaders were united together in their determination to point the world in a new direction, and in the success of this second Assisi initiative, a major step forward was taken. Some days after this historic day, during his Angelus message to the faithful in St. Peter's Square, the pope referred to Assisi II as representing an important advance toward a Civilization of Love.[35] Both Assisi events will be positively evaluated by historians as they bear fruit in our common future.

SOME PERSONAL COMMENTS OF JOHN PAUL II ON BUDDHISM, ISLAM, AND JUDAISM

Normally, popes do not write personal works; they are always related to their office, their universal ministry as the supreme pastor of the Catholic Church, and a major voice in the discourse of the world. Vittorio Messori, an Italian journalist, was granted the rare opportunity of formulating a number of questions for the pope, and he set to answering them in writing. This became his *Crossing the Threshold of Hope*,[36] his reflection on the human reality, the mystery of life and God, the place of Christ, the church, and the necessity for faith. In the course of formulating his reflections, he turned to a brief consideration of the other religions, notably Buddhism, Islam, and Judaism.

Crossing the Threshold of Hope devotes only twenty-three pages to the other religions, basically only scratching the surface of their meaning. The pope regards them from his perspective as a Christian, and his views are not always as refined and developed as they could be. In regarding Buddhism, Islam, and Judaism, he is filtering them through his Christian vision and Catholic theological perspective. Even though these are the pope's personal views, he constantly returns to *Nostra Aetate* as his starting point for guidance in determining his response to each of these traditions and how they measure up in relationship to the Catholic faith.

The pope realizes that Buddhism offers a view of salvation, like Christianity, but unlike Christianity, Buddhism's approach to salvation depends on the individual's own effort, not on God as an external source of grace and redemption itself. In Christian theology, the doctrine of salvation comes under the branch called *soteriology*, which is concerned with the study of the nature of salvation. The pontiff regards Buddhist soteriology as essentially limited because it leaves God out of the picture; thus, its notion of the spiritual life falls short of what is necessary for actual salvation. He comments, "*The Buddhist doctrine of salvation* constitutes the central point, or rather the only point, of this system. Nevertheless, both the Buddhist tradition and the methods deriving from it have an almost exclusively *negative soteriology.*"[37] In relation to the Christian understanding of salvation, with its dependence on Christ and grace, Buddhism's approach seems negative. The pope's comments here were not serenely received by the Buddhist tradition and in fact were harshly criticized by some in that faith.

The pope expresses great respect and admiration for Islam, and he looks to the common ground that unites Christianity and Islam in monotheism. He admires the Muslim commitment to prayer but is not impressed with its reinterpretation of Revelation, which the pope regards as objectively a distortion of the nature of Old and New Testament revelation. He observes by way of evaluation, "Whoever knows the Old and New Testaments, and then reads the Koran, clearly sees the *process by which it completely reduces Divine Revelation.* . . . In Islam all the richness of God's self-revelation, which constitutes the heritage of the Old and New Testaments, has definitely been set aside."[38] He views Islam as essentially a distortion of Judeo-Christian revelation.

When the pope comes to consider the Jewish tradition, there is a sense of coming home. He greatly appreciates the Jewish experience, especially the biblical tradition. He discerns a natural affinity between Christians and Jews. He tells us that he has always had a respect for this great faith and a number of Jewish friends—one in particular, Jerzy Kluger, a Polish Jew, whom he has known all his life and sees him from time to time. The pontiff's great admiration for the Jewish people stems in some measure from his experience of friendship with Jerzy. This relationship put a human face to the Jews for him. His great sense of affection for them, as we saw earlier, has its origin here.

His consideration of the Jewish tradition always refers to the biblical common ground the two faiths share. In addition to this common ground, however, there is a solidarity in suffering and a partnership in the moral activity of recalling the Holocaust. He is able to identify profoundly with the source of their suffering and knows that we are one with them in their vulnerability. He says:

> this was also a personal experience of mine, an experience I carry with me even today. Auschwitz, perhaps the most meaningful symbol of the *Holocaust of the Jewish people*, shows to what lengths a system constructed on principles of racial hatred and greed for power can go. To this day, Auschwitz does not cease to admonish, remind-

ing us that *anti-Semitism is a great sin against humanity*, that all racial hatred inevitably leads to the trampling of human dignity.[39]

In his own theological reflection on the biblical revelation and the place of the Jews—what they have suffered and what they contribute to the world, to culture, and to the church—he has come to the insight that the Jews are "our *elder brothers in the faith*."[40] It is this conviction that informs all his actions in relation to the Jews. We will have occasion to return to this people in the next chapter.

5

THE OFFICIAL MAGISTERIAL
TEACHING OF THE CATHOLIC
CHURCH ON INTERRELIGIOUS
ENCOUNTER AND DIALOGUE

So many factors influence the pope and the Magisterium, which is the pope with the whole Vatican bureaucracy in its teaching function: Scripture, tradition, theological reflection, initiatives in progress, persuasive thinkers, vast experience with members of other religions, the mystical experience of the people involved, the historical circumstances of the times, and the living situation of persons of various faiths encountering one another in the workplace, in academic forums, international organizations, and other areas of culture, economy, and travel. These are just the primary ones; there are more still.

The preceding chapter has presented a portrait of John Paul II that has been gleaned by his presence and attitude toward the other religions, his view of dialogue in practice, the enthusiasm of his commitment, and especially by his actions taken in a number of initiatives, which are ongoing. We also have had a brief taste of his understanding of Buddhism, Islam, and Judaism.

In this pivotal chapter, we will examine the development of the Catholic Church's teaching from Vatican II to the present. We will present some of the contributions of the papal Magisterium and in relation to the council's documents related to interfaith matters. Papal encyclicals of John Paul II and the *Catechism of the Catholic Church* will be explored, as well as documents of other departments of the Vatican Curia, notably the PCID, the Congregation for the Doctrine of the Faith (CDF), and the Commission on Religious Relations with the Jews. Finally, this chapter will consider in some depth the Catholic Church's relationship with the Jewish people as a special case.

VATICAN II AND THE PAPAL
MAGISTERIUM OF JOHN PAUL II

Previously we have noted John Paul's faithfulness to the guidance of Vatican II and to his predecessors, especially Paul VI, in developing his own understanding of and teachings on relations with all the other religions. His view of this important relationship is in harmony with all that went before; and through his presence, example, and articulation of the church's understanding, it will determine consistency in the mind of the church and in those who will follow him in the Apostolic See of Peter. In this sense, popes cannot deviate too much from tradition, though they can formulate a vision of the Catholic Church in its relationship with the realities of this world in a fresh way.

John Paul's commitment to the path of interreligious dialogue, particularly its internal connection to evangelization, shows how much he is in agreement with the evolving tradition of the council on these matters. Of course *Nostra Aetate* has greatly informed the pope's theological and pastoral reflection, and it has also deeply affected how he views his role in relation to the church encountering other faiths. This pontiff often refers to *Nostra Aetate* in his official writings and speeches, in homilies, and in his messages during the Angelus. Moreover, he frequently mentions it in his personal thoughts encompassed in *Crossing the Threshold of Hope*. A commitment to this tradition forms the basis of his own teachings, and the hundreds of statements he has made on the church's relationship to other faiths.

All this pope has said and will say takes its fundamental orientation from *Nostra Aetate*. It is the charter, if you will, of the Catholic Church's policy of engagement with the other world religions. It is the first of many documents, but one that has come to have immense authority in justifying the church's mission beyond its flock. The essence of the church's attitude, as noted earlier, is expressed in this clear directive of Vatican II in *Nostra Aetate*: "Let Christians, while witnessing to their own faith and way of life, acknowledge, preserve and encourage the spiritual and moral truths found among non-Christians, also their social life and culture."[1] What's extraordinary about this statement is how it summarizes the church's essential policy of balancing interreligious dialogue, or outreach to the other faiths, and evangelization; the two goals are present right from the beginning of the change of direction of the church in its regard of the non-Christian faiths.

This change, and the balance between acceptance of the other faiths, while firmly holding to its commitment of its missionary mandate to preach the Gospel to all nations, is echoed in *Lumen Gentium*, which is the *Dogmatic Constitution on the Church*, on the nature and mission of the church, another conciliar document weaved into John Paul's approach. The church regards itself as the sacrament of salvation because it is the sacrament of Christ. It is a vehicle for uniting humankind in God. As *Lumen Gentium* puts it, "the Church, in Christ, is the nature of a sacrament—a sign and instrument, that is, of communion with God and of unity among all men."[2] *Nostra Aetate* has an optimism about salvation outside the church but a certainty of salvation within. As much as the church opens to members of other traditions, it constantly returns to its essential mission: "The Church always held and continues to hold that Christ out of infinite love freely underwent suffering and death because of the sins of all men so that all might attain salvation. It is the duty of the Church, therefore, in her preaching to proclaim the cross of Christ as the sign of God's universal love and the source of all grace."[3] It is necessary to recognize that Catholicism is sincere in this conviction, and so its espousal of everyone's salvation is an expression of a purity of intention and a high expression of love.

Lumen Gentium emphatically proclaims that everyone may be saved if, in their conscience, they are open to the truth. Here the church means members of other faiths who know little of the Catholic tradition and its teachings. There is a trust in divine grace operative in the deepest being of these persons. There is a kind of tacit acknowledgment of the legitimacy of these other faith traditions as a means to carry the conscious intention of their followers in seeking God and the truth. *Lumen Gentium* clarifies: "Those who, through no fault of their own, do not know the Gospel of Christ or his Church, but who nevertheless seek God with a sincere heart, and moved by grace, try in their actions to do his will as they know it through the dictates of their conscience—those too may achieve eternal salvation."[4]

A respect is expressed for the workings of conscience, which is also evidence of the Divine Presence at work in the lives of members of other traditions. These people, in their own way, are pleasing to God, who cannot but reward their sincerity and love. How could they not be inspired since they are "moved by grace"? Divine grace works in all hearts in some mysterious form. In this way and given this theological logic, grace has a certain ubiquity that transcends the direct mediation of the church in those situations where the church has little or no influence. This kind of subtlety and nuancing of the council entered into Paul VI's teachings and those of his successor, John Paul II.

The respect for the conscience of each person extends to everyone in the church's understanding. The individual, no matter his or her tradition, is free; their conscience can follow their convictions or their search for the truth. In Vatican II's document *Dignitatis Humanae*, on religious freedom, the council fathers recognized the absolute right of each individual to freedom of religion, to search for the truth, to seek the Divine Presence. This is not a right granted by the state but innate in us as persons. It is constitutional to our nature, inherent in the dignity of being a human being. Part of that dignity is freedom itself or free will. This dignity and freedom are given by God. *Dignitatis Humanae* states, "The Vatican Council declares that the human person has a right to religious freedom . . . [and] further declares that the right to religious freedom is based in the very dignity of the human person as known through the revealed Word of God and by reason itself."[5] Revelation and our natural intellect lead us to the realization that we are free, or have free will, and this special right is intrinsic to our nature. That being the case, nothing can tamper with our freedom or force us to assent unless we embrace a certain course of faith, action, or being.

Freedom of conscience, or free will, obligates us to seek the truth, to search for God. Freedom carries with it responsibility, a moral imperative to work our way into a clarity about faith, however one decides. The church acknowledges the sacredness of religious freedom, the undetermined will, that no government, organization, individual can manipulate or negate. That includes the Catholic Church as well. The document goes on to tell us how important conscience is in the human journey:

> It is through his conscience that man sees and recognizes the demands of the divine law. He is bound to follow his conscience faithfully in all his activity so that he may come to God, who is his last end. Therefore, he must not be forced to act contrary to his conscience. Nor must he be prevented from acting according to his conscience, especially in religious matters.[6]

The church leaders commit the Catholic community and culture to the supremacy of conscience.

This decree of Vatican II represents a major step forward in Catholicism's relationship with other traditions, since it recognizes the absolute value, primacy, and inviolability of religious freedom and conscience, especially the unmolested exercise of the person's conscience. Although the church wishes to inform its non-Christian interlocutors of the truth and wisdom of the Gospel, it also respects the right of these others to their own faith commitment, to which their own conscience presumably brings them.

The Catholic Church is aware of a great treasure it wishes to share with everyone: the mystery of the Incarnate Son of God. Its commitment to religious liberty, and therefore to dialogue, is unshakable and sincerely held. It is not part of a strategy to woo members of other traditions by entering into a close relationship with their faiths, but rather an expression of an openness of heart to all that is. Ever-mindful of its nature and mission, the church proclaims in *Gaudium et Spes* (Joy and Hope), reiterating what it has said in *Lumen Gentium*, that it is "the universal sacrament of salvation."[7] It knows in faith that it is a light to the world, and it is so eager to share what it knows about why we are here in this world and what is our ultimate destiny. The church has a special knowledge and an urgent task. It is not interested in endless debates about the truth but in genuine, heartfelt dialogue, a dialogue that is all-inclusive, that leaves no one out.[8]

John Paul II, as we have seen briefly in chapter 2, builds solidly on the council's clear guidance and teaching, reaffirming with enthusiasm the necessity and value of interreligious dialogue, but also the mission of the Catholic Church *ad gentes*—that is, to all nations and peoples, indeed, to all the other religions. This vision of its mission, with its origin in its apostolic mandate from Christ himself, to which the church remains ever faithful, guides it in all times, places, and situations. It is the ultimate principle of its relationship with all the religions who are associated with it or seek such an association.

Following the teaching of the council, John Paul is keenly aware of the Holy Spirit's activity in the other traditions. He has often spoken of this insight in many forums and on virtually every continent of the planet. Both the council and the pope regard the activity of the Spirit in the religions and in the depths of all people as a spreading of the seeds of faith in the Word—that is, in Jesus Christ. In his encyclical *Redemptoris Missio* (The Mission of Redemption), the pontiff elaborates:

> The Spirit manifests himself in a special way in the Church, and in her members. Nevertheless, his presence and activity are universal, limited neither by space nor time. . . . The Second Vatican Council recalls that the Spirit is at work in the heart of every person. . . . The Spirit's presence and activity affect not only individuals but also society and history, peoples, cultures and religions.[9]

The Holy Spirit is not a passive observer of human affairs but always intimating himself in everything and in everyone as the prompting of wisdom and inspiration. The Spirit scatters the seeds of faith and spiritual life in all directions. For this reason, the church must pay careful attention to the other religions, discerning this activity of the Spirit in them and an indication of the divine plan in all of this development beyond Christianity. The pope points out that there are two levels of respect the church has in its encounters with other faiths: a respect for the human person seeking the meaning of life, and a respect for the presence and activity of the Holy Spirit in the person.[10]

This reverence for the Spirit at work in the other religions, and so, for those traditions themselves, is a knowledge, or a faith that the Spirit is preparing the ground in the hearts of non-Christians to receive the gift of faith in Jesus. Speaking precisely to this point, the pontiff restates what is a long-maintained theological view of the Catholic Church:

> This is the same Spirit who was at work in the Incarnation and in the life, death and resurrection of Jesus, and who is at work in the Church. He is therefore not an alternative to Christ. . . . Whatever the Spirit brings about in human hearts and in the history of people, in cultures and religions serves as a preparation for the Gospel . . . and can only be understood in reference to Christ.[11]

In the *Catechism of the Catholic Church*, which was approved by the pontiff in June 1992, this preparation for the Gospel is seen to be ontological, intrinsic to our nature. Each one of us is created by God to enjoy communion with him. We are inwardly coordinated to the Divine, to seek the Presence, the Divine One. Everyone has this desire for the Divine, either consciously embracing it or unconsciously exploring it. This is the common ground to begin with, and the *Catechism* clarifies this ontological truth, saying, "The desire for God is written in the human heart, because man is created by God and for God; and God never ceases to draw man to himself."[12] We human beings have a longing for the Divine, and this is constitutional to our nature as persons; it is what defines us in an ultimate sense. The church understands the depth of commitment in the other religions to uncover the mystery of the Divine in human life and aligns itself with this universal and personal task. The *Catechism* continues: "The Catholic Church recognizes in other religions that search, among shadows and images, for the God who is unknown yet near since he gives life and breath to all things, and wants all men to be saved."[13] Again, this desire—indeed, longing—to know and to make contact with God is inspired by the Holy Spirit actively prompting persons in the very depths of their consciousness and moving within their consciences. Everyone makes a stand one way or the other.

The church, through its missionary activity, appeals to this deep desire in the human in preaching the Gospel to non-Christians. A sensitivity is required in evangelization in encountering people who know nothing of the Gospel or even have rejected it. It requires a different approach than would normally be the case. It demands what the *Catechism* calls "a *respectful dialogue.*"[14] This would be one that would not alienate by criticizing their faith or beliefs and that appreciated their customs, culture, symbols, and insights into life.

The *Catechism* refers to harvesting in the missions what the Spirit has accomplished in persons of other faiths. It says that Christians "proclaim the Good News to those who do not know it. In order to consolidate, complete and raise up the truth and the goodness that God has distributed among men and nations."[15] They build on the faith present in these people in other traditions and benefit from what the Spirit has done to open their hearts to receive the eternal Word, or Christ. There doesn't seem to be much concern for preserving the seeds of the Word present in the awareness of non-Christians, though it may be implied in the recommendation of following a "respectful dialogue."

In John Paul's encyclical *Tertio Millennio Adveniente* (On Preparation for the Third Millennium), the pope advances the fulfillment doctrine, which is the official teaching of the Catholic Church regarding the other religions (there will be more on this approach in the next chapter). The religions all have truth in them, but they find their completion in the reality of Christ, the divine Word. He says, "The incarnate Word is . . . the fulfillment of the yearning present in all the religions of mankind: this fulfillment is brought about by God himself and transcends all human expectations. It is the mystery of grace."[16]

This theological doctrine of the church underlies all the conversations it has with members of the other religions. The church is always aware of this insight. Speaking to the PCID membership on November 13, 1992, the pope mentions that in the various forums of dialogue in which the Catholic Church participates, it is seeking to understand the long conversation between the Divine and humankind in all the religious traditions. He expresses it in this way: "Interreligious dialogue at its deepest level is always a *dialogue of salvation*, because it seeks to discover, clarify and understand better the signs of the age-long dialogue which God maintains with mankind."[17] From the perspective of the Catholic tradition, all dialogue involves the focus on salvation, something that deeply concerns the church in every age.

One of the most important teachings of the church on dialogue was issued jointly by the PCID and the Congregation for Evangelization of Peoples on May 19, 1991. *Dialogue and Proclamation* is the most developed and highly detailed teaching of the Catholic tradition thus far on interreligious relations. It is very clear about the nature and role of the church vis-à-vis the whole world, and the members of other traditions, and how the church should relate to them. This significant teaching of the Vatican considers both values and commitments of the church: its mission to proclaim the Gospel to all people, and openness, respect, and mutual exploration of one another's faith.

Many factors make this clarification necessary: the development of contemporary life, with the breakdown of the barriers between and among cultures; instant communication; mass travel; the exchange of ideas; the growing urgency of interfaith encounter; collaborations for peace, justice, and the promotion of environmental awareness; the necessity to stop a new arms race; the positive effects of Assisi I, which demonstrated a unity of purpose and effort on the part of the religions with the church to impact the movement toward a universally peaceful world, and the collective responsibility to collaborate together for that ultimate realization; and the constant encouragement, example, spirit, and presence of Pope John Paul. All of these factors contribute to the need for this document.

The document spends a considerable amount of space defining its terms: *evangelization, dialogue,* and *proclamation.* The ecclesial term *evangelization* is regarded as a more general word to name the Catholic's Church overarching mission. It states, "*Evangelizing mission*, or more simply *evangelization*, refers to the mission of the Church in its totality."[18] The term *dialogue* is used in a precise sense to refer to the whole situation of religious diversity in which enlightened relationships are being pursued through persons and groups of members of the religions in conversation with the church. It emphasizes interfaith relations that are oriented to building bonds between the church and these other communities in a spirit of mutual benefit and understanding, promoting a deeper relationship and open to freedom and the larger picture of truth.[19]

Dialogue is a very rich term, as complex and multidimensional as the reality it represents, and as variegated as the actors in any dialogical process. Here, in this teaching, the Catholic Church is focused on a more general goal: creating the environment of trust, mutual respect, and a sense of human solidarity to pursue the truth together in an atmosphere of freedom and honesty about the faith commitments of the interlocutors. Dialogue requires a culture of warmth, friendliness, safety, and comfort, which allows the participants to share authentically from the depths of their conviction, experience, and hope. *Dialogue and Proclamation* attempts to encourage these qualities in the dialogical situation and process.

The word *proclamation* has a much more precise meaning than *evangelization*, in this context; it means the dissemination of the truth of the Good News, the Gospel. As the document expresses it, "*Proclamation* is the communication of the Gospel message, the mystery of salvation realized by God for all in Jesus Christ by the power of the Spirit. It is an invitation to a commitment of faith in Jesus Christ and to entry through baptism into the community of believers which is the Church."[20] This clear and emphatic statement articulates with a certain finality the nonnegotiable bottom line of the Catholic Church's self-understanding of its mission, what it means in terms of the rest of the world, especially in relation to the other religions. It is not a matter the church is willing to tamper with, modify, or even qualify, since it has a very precise goal in mind: sharing the truth about Jesus Christ, the Incarnate Son of God. Naturally, this affects the church's understanding of dialogue itself and its relations with the other religions. In this document, the church is being blunt in its honesty.

Dialogue and Proclamation reaffirms the teaching of the council, especially as announced in *Lumen Gentium* 48, that the church is the universal sacrament of salvation. It is an instrument of salvation and has the responsibility to share the Good News with everyone. Since the church has the mandate from Christ to pursue evangelization, interreligious dialogue becomes one of the means chosen to advance this goal and is indeed central to its evangelizing mission. It is the cause of salvation for everyone that inspires the church into dialogue with the other religions. The document goes on to clarify:

> The foundation of the Church's commitment to dialogue is not merely anthropological but primarily theological. God, in an age-long dialogue, has offered and continues to offer salvation to humankind. In faithfulness to the divine initiative, the Church too must enter into a dialogue of salvation with all men and women.[21]

The church's interest in dialogue, its embracing of it as a value, practice, and urgent task, has its basis in a theological imperative: spreading the knowledge of salvation in Christ, the Incarnate Son. Although there is a commitment to interreligious dialogue that springs from its interest in human life, or the anthropological concern, the deeper concern is with God's plan for the entire human family, which the church represents in every age and to which it must give constant witness in various ways. After Vatican II, one of the primary ways, other than through its missionary activity, is through dialogue. Interreligious dialogue is thus intimately bound to evangelization and, more specifically, to proclamation.

Dialogue and Proclamation then develops four dispositions necessary for interreligious dialogue: (1) a balanced attitude, (2) religious conviction, (3) openness to truth, and (4) new dimensions of faith.[22] Genuine interfaith conversation, a dialogue of substance, requires a balanced attitude on the part of the participants. First, they must balance a critical attitude with one that is open, having a kind of childlike receptivity and simplicity, a mildness of being.[23] Second, the interlocutors have to maintain the authenticity of their faith in the conversations, while remaining sensitive to God's presence and action in other traditions. The document declares that "the sincerity of interreligious dialogue requires that each enters into it with integrity of his or its own faith [but] . . . Christians must remember that God has also manifested himself in some way to the followers of other religious traditions."[24] Third, those engaged in dialogue have an openness to truth and are able to learn from one another. Their faith can be illumined through the process of dialogue.[25] Fourth, through a spirit and practice of openness in dialogue, positive effects will result, and these are the fruits of dialogue. As the document expresses it: "Far from weakening their [Christians'] own faith, true dialogue will deepen it. . . . Their faith will gain new dimensions as they discover the active presence of the mystery of Jesus Christ beyond the visible boundaries of the Church and of the Christian fold."[26] These qualities are meant to guide Christians and others engaged in conversations across traditions.

OBSTACLES TO DIALOGUE

Just as *Dialogue and Proclamation* enumerates the indispensable dispositions for meaningful and substantive dialogue to occur, particularly as an ongoing process, it also mentions some of the difficulties that can become obstacles to genuine dialogue. These obstacles may involve all traditions, or some of them in special circumstances, but they can be serious enough to derail conversation or block it from happening. These include (1) a lack of "sufficient grounding in one's own faith"; (2) not enough background and understanding of the doctrines, prayer, rituals, and other spiritual practices of the other faiths, and these deficiencies can cause distortions in characterizing those traditions, with considerable misunderstanding; (3) historical, political, social, and economic factors; (4) an inaccurate understanding of words or terms; (5) an attitude of smugness, insufficient openness, a kind of aggressiveness, and defensiveness; (6) a lack of understanding of dialogue's indispensable value and role and regarding it as weakness, and perhaps even of turning one's back on the Christian faith; (7) distrust of the other in conversation and suspicion of his or her motives; (8) a polemical and combative nature in discussions when representing one's religious faith; (9) an attitude of intolerance and the absence of reciprocity in the discussions, often bogging them down in frustration; and, finally, (10) the confusion caused by contemporary cultural features, such as consumerism, entertainment, skepticism, indifference, and a lot of new age groups, new religious sects, all clouding the issues.[27]

All these factors, either alone or in combination, can conspire to make dialogue difficult, if not impossible. Authentic dialogue requires a supportive environment; it needs a culture designed for it to thrive. We have to do the hard work of developing our faith and have a profound inner knowledge of as well as a deep commitment to it in all the situations of life. We have to invest the time for study and reflection of the other's faith tradition, and we must learn to trust our interlocutors. Most of all, we should be comfortable in the dialogical relationship, deriving life from it, and we must be willing to trust the other. Aware of the situation of constant change, we need to attend to the possibility of change in the lives of those with whom we seek conversation. The primary requirement is openness, and that is really the call of the Gospel.

SOME ASPECTS OF CHRISTIAN MEDITATION

Some Aspects of Christian Meditation is a declaration of the CDF of October 15, 1989, addressed to all the bishops of the Catholic Church. It has occasioned considerable controversy both within the church and beyond because it seemed to signal a shift back to the past. In chapter 7, we will look at some of the reactions to this pronouncement. There can be no doubt that the document is a strong reaction against what is perceived as an encroaching Eastern influence, notably from certain Hindu and Buddhist practices relating to meditation.

Many complaints over the years leading to the promulgation of the document express concern by some of the faithful, bishops, priests, and superiors of religious orders about this growing influence, which some have perceived as a threat to the identity of Christians and to the faith itself. The document is, in many ways, a response to this concern, a concern shared by Rome. *Some Aspects of Christian Meditation* is an attempt to clear up confusion and ambiguity about what is acceptable in prayer and what is not. It is meant to present guidelines to assist Christians in their spiritual lives. It should be remarked at the outset that the document is very Western and, more narrowly, presents a Eurocentric theological view; that is, it is conceived in the terms of Western Christianity with its European language sources, especially Latin, Greek, French, German, Italian, and Spanish. Again, I will have more to say on this point in chapter 7.

This whole area of discussion really comes under the category of the dialogue of the heart and even the dialogue of life, which are both deeply existential in character. The context is, therefore, a kind of shared practice, which is normally how an introduction into these Eastern forms of prayer occur. These shared moments happen in a number of forums: retreats, workshops, symposia, seminars, conferences, regular programs of teachers in which initiation might occur, and formal interfaith dialogues. These represent the disseminating vehicles of such methods of prayer, particularly of meditation in its various forms.

In *Some Aspects*, the CDF describes the general context that occasioned this clarifying teaching document. It mentions the deep desire many Christians have to experience deeper levels of prayer and how this desire has led some to use Eastern forms or to experiment with these on an ongoing basis. Their longing is to know the contemplative rest of the mystics and the possibility of intimacy with God. The CDF instruction wants to ensure that the focus in prayer is decisively Christ-centric. Here is its introductory formulation:

> Many Christians today have a keen desire to experience a deeper and authentic prayer life despite the considerable difficulties which modern culture places in the way of the need for silence, recollection and meditation. The interest which in recent years has been awakened also among some Christians by forms of meditation associated with some Eastern religions and their particular methods of prayer is a significant sign of this need for spiritual recollection and a deep contact

with the divine mystery. Nevertheless, faced with this phenomenon many feel the need for sure criteria of a doctrinal and pastoral character which might allow them to instruct others in prayer, in its numerous manifestations, while remaining faithful to the truth revealed in Jesus, by means of the genuine tradition of the Church. This present letter seeks to reply to this urgent need.[28]

There is a protective motive here to allow the Catholic Church to sit back and examine this influx of influence from the East and guide Christians about the risks and dangerous involved in such explorations, always drawing attention to what is genuine prayer in its Christian understanding. The letter points out that Christians engaged in these other forms of prayer are wondering what value these non-Christian kinds of prayer have for them and others.[29] Some are attracted to these forms but need guidance about them in relation to prayer in the Catholic tradition.

This document strongly advises that all prayer be essentially Christ-centric, that it be oriented to Christ, who is the culmination of revelation. The letter declares, "There exists . . . a strict relationship between revelation and prayer. . . . This revelation takes place through words and actions which have a constant mutual reference, one to the other; from the very beginning everything proceeds to converge on Christ, the fullness of revelation and grace."[30] Through prayer, one becomes more intimately aligned with Jesus Christ and his Father in the Holy Spirit. All prayer, in the letter's view, must consciously intend Christ and a relationship with him, his Spirit and the Father, the Source.

It is because the Catholic Church wishes to encourage this kind of Trinitarian prayer, to shed light on how all prayer involves the Three Persons of the Godhead and leads to intimacy with the Trinity, that it encourages the faithful to read Sacred Scripture on a regular basis. Doing so, their prayer life is nourished from an authentic source of wisdom. The document states, "[T]he Church recommends the reading of the Word of God as a source of Christian prayer, and at the same time exhorts all to discover the deep meaning of Sacred Scripture through prayer."[31] Furthermore, the constant context of Christian prayer is the prayer of Jesus, which the Church holds in trust and has a mandate to guard. The prayer of each person should be expressed within this context in union with Christ and his Church. The letter remarks by way of clarification: "The Christian, even when he is alone and prays in secret, is conscious that he always prays for the good of the Church in union with Christ, in the Holy Spirit and together with all the saints."[32]

Some Aspects of Christian Meditation refers to dangers in trying to integrate Christian prayer with Hindu or Buddhist forms of meditation practice. It suggests this can be both confusing and misleading, since it distracts from the properly Christ-centric nature of prayer in the Catholic tradition, including prayer in other communions of the Christian tradition. It is accepting of these methods as preparations for genuine contemplation in Christian mysticism. It goes on to warn against syncretism, a kind of forced synthesis or integration of methods. It calls for careful scrutinization of these methods to avoid such syncretism.[33]

The letter tells us that Christians can learn from the forms of prayer or methods of meditation and the mystical life in other religions, but they must maintain the Christian understanding of prayer, its inner coherence and conditions. We may borrow from these other forms, but we must not lose our sense of identity. The document expresses it succinctly: "[O]ne can take from them [the other religions] what is useful so long as the Christian conception of prayer, its logic and requirements, are never obscured."[34] The church is open to sharing and comparing, but not substituting non-Christian elements for Christian ones.

The document emphasizes that Christian prayer is not a technique but a relationship with God, and it does not wish to see this relationship obscured, modified, or lessened in any way. We cannot make the mystical life happen simply by our own efforts. So much of it is given to us when the Divine so chooses. In an eloquent sentence, the letter sums up the difference, by implication, between Eastern methods of prayer and mystical experience and Christian contemplation. It pointedly says, "Genuine Christian mysticism has nothing to do with technique: it is always a gift of God; and the one who benefits from it knows himself to be unworthy."[35] It states further that Eastern methods may be quite useful in our process of inner growth, but again, they have to seen in the context of Christian prayer.

DOMINUS IESUS

On September 5, 2000, the CDF, with the preceding approval of the pontiff on June 16, 2000, promulgated "the Declaration *Dominus Iesus* on the Unicity and Salvific Universality of Jesus Christ and the Church."[36] This declaration stirred up a storm of controversy within the Catholic Church, the other churches, and the other religions. In chapter 7, we will return to *Dominus Iesus* in this context. Here I wish only to convey the substance of the document vis-à-vis the other traditions of faith and the other Christian communities of faith.

Essentially, *Dominus Iesus* is meant to clarify and reaffirm the Catholic Church's teaching on the unique salvific place of Christ and his Church as the instrument of salvation in the world. The CDF felt compelled to issue this corrective in the light of the movement of pluralism (i.e., the notion that all the religions are on an equal footing, thus relativizing the Catholic Church's claim to ultimacy). *Dominus Iesus* declares:

> The Church's constant missionary proclamation is endangered today by relativistic theories which seek to justify religious pluralism, not only de facto but also de iure [or in principle]. As a consequence, it is held certain truths have been superseded; for example, the definitive and complete character of the revelation of Jesus Christ, the nature of Christian faith as compared with that of belief in other religions, the inspired nature of the Sacred Scripture, the personal unity between the Eternal Word and Jesus of Nazareth, the unity of the economy of the Incarnate Word and the Holy Spirit, the Unicity and salvific universality of the mystery of Jesus Christ, the universal salvific meditation of the Church, the inseparability—while recognizing the distinction—of the kingdom of God, the kingdom of Christ, and the Church, and the subsistence of the one Church of Christ in the Catholic Church.[37]

It should be clear that the faith of the Catholic Church is infinitely deep and its commitment to Christ is absolute. It takes its role with great seriousness and subordinates everything to it. It is single-minded about its mission, and this declaration is meant to clarify its commitment. This particular passage illustrates the depth of the church's understanding of its mission, and it clearly is the lens through which it pursues interreligious dialogue.

Again, the church discerns the presence of the Spirit at work in all the religions and has great respect for them, but it is also aware that ultimately the aspirations of the religions are fulfilled in Christ and thus in the church itself. The Catholic Church sees itself as necessary for salvation, a vehicle to guide people on the path to ultimate beatitude. Salvation is available to everyone via the mysterious grace of Christ, even though the persons of other traditions are outside the visible structures of the church.[38] These other religions have truth and moral values, but according to the church's understanding, they lack the means of salvation. *Dominus Iesus* sums the matter up in this way: "If it is true that the followers of other religions can receive divine grace, it is also certain that objectively speaking they are in a gravely deficient situation in comparison with those who, in the Church, have the fullness of the means of salvation."[39] It is this conviction, nourished by the New Testament and the testimony of the apostolic age, that guides the church in every age, and especially as it encounters the rich diversity of faiths everywhere.

THE SPECIAL RELATIONSHIP OF THE CATHOLIC CHURCH WITH THE JEWISH PEOPLE

When considering the example of John Paul II in chapter 4, there was a brief consideration of his own personal relationship with the Jews. He has had lifelong friendships with Jews from Poland and has made other bonds in the years of his pontificate. This is a pontiff personally committed and guiding the Catholic Church into a similar irrevocable bond of relationship with the Jewish people. Returning to his interventions during his historic visit to the chief synagogue of Rome on April 13, 1986, the pope refers to the desire to cultivate the bond further and deeper. He comments on the evolving relationship and the purpose of his visit:

> Today's visit is meant to make a decisive contribution to the consolidation of the good relations between our two communities, in imitation of the example of so many men and women who have worked and who are still working today, on both sides, to overcome old prejudices and to secure ever wider and fuller recognition of that "bond" and that "common spiritual patrimony" that exists between Jews and Christians.[40]

The pope goes on to elucidate the spiritual nature of this bond, unique between Jews and Christians, and unlike any other relationship the Catholic Church has with non-Christian religions. Quoting liberally from *Nostra Aetate* 4, he locates the foundation of the relationship in the biblical experience of the Jews and their covenant with God commencing at the time of Abraham. He mentions how influential paragraph 4 of *Nostra Aetate* was and is in providing a direction for the church in the development of relations with the Jewish community around the world. He comments, "The decisive turning-point in relations between the Catholic Church and Judaism, and with individual Jews, was occasioned by this brief but incisive paragraph."[41] In this paragraph he identifies three essential points he wishes to emphasize for their far-reaching implications and their impact on the future course of relations.

The first [point] is that the Church discovers its "bond" with Judaism
by "searching into its own mystery" (*NA* [*Nostra Aetate*] 4). The Jewish religion is not "extrinsic" to us, but in a certain way is "intrinsic"
to our own religion. With Judaism, therefore, we have a relationship
which we do not have with any other religion.... The second point
noted by the Council is that no ancestral or collective blame can be
imputed to the Jews as a people for "what happened in Christ's passion" [*NA* 4]....

[T]he third point ... [is that] it is not lawful to say that the Jews
are "repudiated or cursed," as if this is taught or could be deduced
from the Sacred Scriptures of the Old and New Testaments [*NA* 4].[42]

This visit, its focus and its clear direction in terms of forging the
new relationship, has had an enormous impact, since it was symbolically
healing but substantially profound in its spiritual teaching about the biblical roots of the special relationship that exists between Jews and Christians. It is, furthermore, practically, culturally, and theologically significant
because of the spiritual bond but also because of the second and third
points, the exoneration of blame and the dismantling of the repudiation
and curses traditionally applied to the Jewish people. This pope and his
predecessors have labored diligently to deconstruct the culture of anti-
Judaism or its more virulent type, anti-Semitism, in the Catholic
Church. This is a story still to be told more fully to the larger populations of the world and that would serve as an example of deep reconciliation, friendship, and love for everyone.

To underscore the utter seriousness of this pope's and the Catholic
Church's extraordinary commitment to the new course and the relationship with the people of the first covenant, the pontiff approved the
long-awaited document of the Vatican's Commission for Religious Relations with the Jews on March 12, 1998. This very significant statement
is entitled *We Remember: A Reflection on the Shoah*.[43] In a letter attached
to the document and addressed to Cardinal Edward Idris Cassidy, the
president of the commission and the chief signatory of the *Reflection*,
John Paul says, "It is my hope that the document ... will indeed help to
heal the wounds of past misunderstandings and injustices. May it enable
memory to play its necessary part in the process of shaping a future in
which the unspeakable iniquity of the *Shoah* will never again be possible."[44]

It is clear to see from this pope's example and guidance, as well as
from this important document and the hard work of other Christians,
that the Catholic Church holds the Holocaust very close to its heart, that

its expressions around it are profoundly serious. This *Reflection* binds the church in a solemn way to its new relationship with the Jewish community. The tone and substance of the document, and especially its implications, indicate that the church, since Vatican II and, really, since World War II, has been considering what Christians have contributed to this historic tragedy. The document calls upon Christians to reflect on our history and our responsibility. It mentions how the Holocaust happened in Christian Europe.[45] It refers to the statement of Pope Pius IX, who eloquently declared, "Spiritually, we are all Semites."[46] Although the *Reflection* does not blame Christians for the generation of anti-Semitism, it does say that the church did encourage what it calls an anti-Judaism, which is more a religious prejudice and was never a form of racism.[47] There can be no doubt that the relationship is getting closer and closer, which is expressed in this way: "[T]he Jews are our dearly beloved brothers [and sisters], indeed in a certain sense they are 'our elder brothers.'"[48] I believe the change is a permanent one and the basis of the development of similar bonds with members of other traditions.

Part III

CONTRADICTIONS IN THE UNDERSTANDING OF THE CHURCH

6

THE THREE BASIC
POSITIONS ON THE OTHER
RELIGIOUS TRADITIONS

The Catholic Church's perception of the other world religions has gone through quite an evolution in the past two thousand years. Until the seventeenth century, the church had little experience of encountering the other religions. In those centuries, the church and these religious traditions were really cultures of isolation, essentially ignorant of one another. The early experience of the Christian community was primarily confined to the Jews, and this relationship was not very positive. Later, Christians had a very negative experience with Islam for centuries, with so much blood spilled. The church had little contact with Hinduism, Buddhism, Jainism, Taoism, and the lesser traditions until the seventeenth century. These encounters were mostly in the context of its missionary activity. Naturally, cultural isolation and the mutual ignorance of one another's traditions contributed to the negative perceptions and misrepresentations of the other religions in the church's view of these faiths.

Since these earlier experiences and misunderstandings, the Catholic Church has gained considerable understanding of the various world religions. As its knowledge has increased and its understanding has become more subtle, its perception and view of the other traditions has undergone a profound change. We will examine this change, and the new perspective, which has become the church's official position.

We have seen in the preceding chapters the Catholic Church's clear position on the other religions. It can be said, in historical terms, that this position enunciated by the pontiff, other church authorities in various forums from Vatican II onward, and countless documents of the Holy See represents a middle way, what is called *inclusivism*, between two extremes: those of *exclusivism*, on the conservative right in the past, and *pluralism*, on the left, the view of theological liberals on the matter of the Catholic Church's relationship to the non-Christian traditions. In this chapter we will examine in some detail these three positions.

EXTRA ECCLESIAM NULLA SALUS: THE BASIS OF EXCLUSIVISM

The oldest of the three views, exclusivism goes back to the patristic period and represented the Catholic Church's understanding for centuries. Even today its effects can still be discerned in various parts of the world and in some very conservative segments of the church, though they may not speak and write openly in this way. It is clearly the sentiment of a minority who have never really accepted the opening to the other traditions or the possibility of real dialogue with representatives of these traditions. Of course, this is no longer the official view of the Catholic Church, which we will see in the following section on inclusivism.

The exclusivist proposition can be formulated in this way: Salvation, or eternal beatitude with God, with the Trinity, angels, and saints, is only possible in and through the mediation of the Catholic Church and those in union or communion with the church. This possibility of salvation is achieved through the salvific act of Jesus Christ through the Redemption that occurred in the Incarnation when he became a human being, while remaining fully divine. This very sober teaching of the Catholic Church has been rendered in a maxim summing up the substance of the position: "*Extra ecclesiam nulla salus,*" or "Outside the church there is no salvation." This has been the view of the Catholic world nearly since the beginning of Christianity, and it has lasted well into the twentieth century, ending only with its abandonment at the Second Vatican Council.[1] Exclusivism's long history was based on the New Testament, more specifically, on a passage from 1 Peter. In this letter, attributed to the apostle Peter himself by tradition, the leader of the church is speaking to a Christian community within the context of baptism. In 1 Peter 3:18–21, the author uses the image of Noah's ark, which becomes an image of the church, and just as the eight in Noah's time were saved through the ark, we are saved through the waters of the sacrament of baptism in the ark of the church. The passage reads:

> Christ himself died once and for all for sins, the upright for the sake of the guilty, to lead us to God. In the body he was put to death, in

the spirit he was raised to life, and, in the spirit, he went to preach to the spirits in prison. They refused to believe long ago, while God patiently waited to receive them, in Noah's time when the ark was being built.

In it only a few, that is eight souls, were saved through water. It is the baptism corresponding to this water which saves you now—not the washing off of physical dirt but the pledge of a good conscience given to God through the resurrection of Jesus Christ.[2]

Peter is drawing a parallel between the ark of Noah, which saved the remnant of humanity at the time of the flood, and the church, the ark of Christ. In Noah's time, the eight were saved *from* the rising waters, while in the ages of Christ, the Incarnate Son, we are saved through his grace in the sacraments, beginning with the baptism, the living waters, and sustained by the Eucharist. Through baptism, in the ark of the church, we are saved *in* these waters of baptism. Commenting on this passage and its meaning, Joseph Osei-Bonsu, an African theologian, reflects on the meaning in terms of salvation and the church. "We should observe that whereas 1 Peter 3:20 states positively that there is salvation *inside* the ark, i.e., in the Church, it does not say there is salvation *only* in the ark; neither does it add the negative statement that there is *no salvation outside the ark.*"[3] This insight is important because it suggests the negative assertion was added without much consideration of Scripture—that is, what 1 Peter actually says or implies; it goes way beyond the genuine meaning and spirit of the passage and really distorts them both by the harsh tone and content it gives it.

Ignatius of Antioch in the second century was the first of the fathers of the church to appropriate the image of the ark, identifying it with the church, though not in the same context as the subsequent tradition—that is, in relation to salvation.[4] In the third century, Clement of Alexandria clearly equated salvation with membership in the church. He regards salvation as part of the commitment to be a disciple of Christ. The very act of following the Incarnate Son is an indication of the person being chosen for salvation. The Divine chooses the church as the instrument of salvation, of spreading it among humankind. Clement declares, "To follow Christ is salvation," and the Divine's "decision is the salvation of human persons and this is called the Church."[5]

It was the great Greek father, Origen, who was to render the maxim in its negative form that has come down to us from his times. Origen explicitly connects salvation to the church and its mission of ministering to souls, saving them from error and sin, which left to their own devices would result. He is quite emphatic about the necessity of the church, its role in promoting the eternal well-being of all souls, if accepted by them. He points out that they can only be saved in the bosom of the church, which protects them from evil forces, from themselves, and from temptations. With devastating clarity and finality, he proclaims the adage that has been the hallmark of the exclusivist view ever since: "Let no one fool himself; outside this house, i.e., outside of the Church, no one is saved; for if someone goes outside, he becomes responsible for his own death."[6]

Also in the third century, Cyprian, the bishop of Carthage in North Africa, popularized this teaching expressed in the negative form of the adage. His interpretation was inflexibly rigorous and harsh. He also regarded the church as necessary for salvation, and one had a responsibility to remain united to it throughout the course of one's earthly sojourn. He says, "Whoever goes out from the gathering, that is, whoever withdraws from the Church, will be guilty, that is, the fact [that] he will perish will be imputed to himself."[7] He was convinced that salvation came through the instrumentality of the church and was not possible for anyone beyond its range. He boldly asserts, "There is no salvation outside the Church."[8]

Augustine of Hippo, fourth to fifth century, probably the most influential theologian in the Christian world and certainly the most formative, did much to defend the exclusivist notion of salvation, as had Cyprian before him. He also popularized this teaching, making it widely known in his time and the ages to follow. There is no doubt in Augustine's mind that the church is indispensable for salvation. Clarifying this for all time, Augustine maintains, "Whoever is separated from this Catholic Church—however much he believes he is living laudably—will not have life but the anger of God rests upon him; the reason is this offense alone: he is sundered from the unity of Christ."[9] The church, as a community of faith, is a communion with God, and it possesses the means of salvation in grace as well as in design. Augustine certainly understood this point very well, but he was also trying to protect the church, as well as the flock, from influences he regarded as inimical to faith. He knew that the church was willed by God and was so arranged in its very depth, structure, teaching, and sacraments to facilitate the salvation of the faithful.

The writings of Origen, Cyprian, and Augustine on this issue seem to lack compassion for the non-Christian, or at least their understanding of salvation needs further nuancing and refinement, something that was not to happen until the time of Thomas Aquinas in the thirteenth century—

the Angelic Doctor, as he came to be called. He became the Catholic Church's philosopher and theologian, dominating the centuries from the thirteenth well into the twentieth.

Aquinas, or St. Thomas, lived in an age, the long medieval period, in which the Catholic Church was committed to the position that salvation could only happen in the church, that it was not possible beyond its domain.[10] He had a more subtle approach. Although he accepted the long-held position of his predecessors, and the church as such, he introduced a new element. He speaks about what he calls *implicit faith* as sufficient for salvation, and he extends this understanding to non-Christians. This implicit faith is in Christ, the Mediator, though they are not explicitly aware of him, nor do they intend him directly. It is rather related to faith in divine providence. This implicit faith opens them to the possibility of salvation. Here is how he expresses this insight in relation to the Gentiles, with great subtlety:

> If, however some [Gentiles] were saved without receiving any revelation, they were not saved without faith in a Mediator, for though they did not believe in Him explicitly, they did, nevertheless, have implicit faith through believing in divine providence, since they believed that God would deliver mankind in whatever way was pleasing to Him, and according to the revelation of the Spirit to those who knew the truth.[11]

There is no doubt that Thomas's teaching represents an advance on earlier views and makes allowances for a pastoral flexibility that takes into account the interior dispositions of non-Christians, especially with respect to the state of their faith itself. It also evidences in Thomas a more profound understanding of God, his ways, and his mercy toward us all, since it uncovers how a simple openness of faith in God's providence is itself sufficient to open the door to eternal beatitude.

The exclusivist position, in a version of its maxim form, was endorsed by papal authority directly during the pontificate of Pope Boniface VIII, who issued the papal bull entitled *Unam Sanctam*, or One Holy (referring to the marks of the church: One, Holy, Catholic, and Apostolic), on November 18, 1302. In this authoritative document, this pope settles the questions as far as the official teaching of the church goes at that time. The bull declares:

> Faith urges and constrains us to believe in and to embrace the One, Holy, Catholic, and Apostolic Church, and we firmly believe and absolutely confess this [Church] outside of which there is neither

salvation nor forgiveness. . . . To be sure at the time of the flood there was one Ark of Noah, a type of the one Church. . . . We read that outside the Ark all living creatures were destroyed.[12]

Although this declaration defines a matter of faith, it was not an infallible statement. If so, it would have been difficult for Vatican II to reverse it in its adoption of an inclusivist position.

Another important event in the history of the axiom of exclusivism, and this whole consciousness in the church, was a statement of the Council of Florence in 1442, which essentially confirmed Boniface VIII's teaching. This council solemnly declared that it was necessary for salvation that Jews, pagans, schismatics (Christians who separate themselves from the church, such as a cult), and heretics must be united to the Catholic Church to be saved, and that salvation was only possible for them, or indeed anyone, in this way.[13] Thus the exclusivist view held sway in this form well into the nineteenth century when a modification was made during the pontificate of Pope Pius IX and was later confirmed by the First Vatican Council (1869–1870).

Pius IX, whose reign was from 1846 to 1878, like Thomas Aquinas, introduced a nuance to the traditional position of the church, a nuance that represented theological flexibility, reflecting the mercy of God, and the pastoral sensitivity of the church. It represented a step forward to a doctrine that was essentially backward in its conception and application. He proclaimed, "Those who are in invincible ignorance of our most holy religion but who carefully observe the natural law and its precepts which God has written in the hearts of all men [all persons], who are ready to obey God and to lead an honest and upright life, can through the power of the divine light and grace attain eternal life."[14] In effect, this further clarification, beyond Thomas though in a sense implied by his theological vision, extends the possibility of salvation to all and actually nullifies *extra ecclesiam nulla salus.*

The First Vatican Council, called by Pius IX and over which he presided (one might observe, every detail of it), expressed in a formal decree the same kind of clarificatory teaching, and it has to be seen as progress in the church's understanding, along with Pope Pius's antecedent action, setting the course for the council and the future direction of the church. Vatican I maintains:

[I]t is a dogma of faith that outside the Church no one can be saved. And yet those who are invincibly ignorant of Christ and his Church must not for this reason be condemned to eternal punishments, for they are not bound by any fault in this matter in the eyes of the Lord, who wishes all men [all persons] to be saved and to come to a knowledge of the truth and who does not deny grace to him who does what is within his power to attain justification and eternal life.[15]

This insight brims with awareness, sensitivity, and compassion, reflecting the awareness, sensitivity, compassion, and mercy of God, the great love of the Divine, the Trinity, as a community of love at the heart of being and in the mystery of the Incarnate Son. Such a view is a huge step forward, but not quite yet the great opening to and welcoming of the other faiths by the church.

Even though Vatican II set aside the old view in favor of the inclusivist approach, in the *Catechism of the Catholic Church*, Rome defends the exclusivist view, even though the catechism was only promulgated in 1992. It defends and reinterprets the axiom. It purports to restate the maxim in a language more acceptable today: "How are we to understand this affirmation, often repeated by the Church Fathers? Reformulated positively, it means that all salvation comes from Christ the Head through the Church which is his Body."[16] Of course, theologically, this restatement is consistent with the long-standing teaching of the church, and to recast it in this form is far less objectionable than the sober tone and content of *extra ecclesiam nulla salus*.

This does not mean that the church no longer believes in its indispensable role as the vehicle of salvation or that this salvation comes through faith, explicit or implicit, in Jesus Christ. It does suggest that the church has changed its way of proclaiming this element of the Catholic vision. John Hick understands well the new situation: "The claim has now come to be expressed in less blatant and less offensive ways. In the modern reaction against the triumphalism of the past the Church's still cherished assumption of Christian superiority has moved discreetly into the background."[17] It is still there, but not voiced in quite the same way, though *Dominus Iesus* would seem to be a return to the spirit of earlier times.

One very important implication of the exclusivist doctrine is that it entails a negative conclusion about the other religions as vehicles of salvation. They have truth and moral values in them, and the church proclaims, preserves, and celebrates these, but it regards the other religions as "gravely deficient" when it comes to the means of salvation, as we saw in the section on *Dominus Iesus*. The other religions are regarded by the church as savifically problematic, since they cannot save on their own, but only through the grace of Christ. Such is the thrust of implication of the exclusivist view.

INCLUSIVISM: REACHING OUT
TO THE WHOLE OF HUMANITY

Rejecting the more narrow view, the Second Vatican Council optimistically envisioned the possibility of salvation outside embracing all of humankind, though the theology of this more welcoming notion is still very much consistent with what the church has always held to with regard to Christ and the church. These truths it sees as nonnegotiable. The implication of the exclusivist proposition dovetails with inclusivism in that the conclusion of the exclusivist argument is part of the inclusivist view, since in either case the church is necessary for salvation.

Gavin D'Costa, a talented theologian devoted to interreligious dialogue from an academic perspective, in his book *Theology and Religious Pluralism*, briefly defines inclusivism, saying that it "affirms the salvific presence of God in non-Christian religions, while still maintaining that Christ is the definitive and authoritative revelation of God."[18] What this means is that God's grace is active in the other religions, inspiring them, prompting them, illuminating them, and granting them special insights, intuitions, mystical, or contemplative experiences, perceptions, or mental elevations into the divine awareness itself or an aspect of it. This means, furthermore, that the Holy Spirit is actively engaged with the members of these traditions, with their saints, mystics, and ordinary faithful. The Spirit dwells in their hearts—that is, in the core depths of their subjectivity, in their openness to the Divine or to the Truth, their questing for it. This activity of the Holy Spirit, of the Father, and of the Son, or Logos, is salvific; it conduces to salvation, the ultimate beatitude of each member of these many faiths scattered around the world and throughout history. God is always working his way in the minds and hearts of everyone, everywhere, and at all times.

Even though this is true, in the inclusive vision of the Catholic Church, the grace of salvation happens through the mediation of Christ. It maintains the fundamental commitment of the Christian faith that Jesus Christ is the definitive, ultimate, and final and fully divine revelation of the Godhead, thus having supreme authority. The activity of the Divine Presence in the other religions and in the minds and hearts of their followers—indeed, of all persons—is one that is oriented toward their realization of the truth of Christ and the Gospel as they evolve in their understanding. The upshot of inclusivism is quite significant, since it says essentially that salvation is open to everyone, regardless of their faith, or not, as long as they are open to truth and are actively living a moral life. This possibility of salvation is the result of Christ's salvific act in the Redemption, in what he achieved for all of us. Inclusivism thus represents the reversal of exclusivism and the rejection of the Christian axiom *extra ecclesiam nulla salus.*

Many Christian thinkers have been inclined adopt the inclusivist view, and figures even in the early church espoused it,[19] but the most influential theologian in generating the necessary awareness in the church, especially at the time of Vatican II, was the German Jesuit thinker, Karl Rahner (1904–1984). His impact on the council was profound and comprehensive. He regarded the Christian faith as the ultimate expression of the Truth and the destiny of the human family, and held that the other traditions, though somewhat inspired by God, were inadequate for the purposes of salvation. Even so, Rahner recognized, along with Vatican II, the existence of truth and moral values, insights, and genuine spiritual experience in these other traditions. The non-Christian traditions, he concluded, were recipients of supernatural grace and divine assistance toward salvation of their members.[20] His insights became substantially part of the emerging tradition emanating from Vatican II.

In *Lumen Gentium,* we discern this attitude of optimism about the possibility of salvation for non-Christians. It is an approach similar to that enunciated by Pius IX and Vatican I, though it is more positive and compassionate in its formulation. *Lumen Gentium* proclaims:

> Those also can attain to everlasting salvation who through no fault of their own do not know the gospel of Christ or His Church, yet sincerely seek God, and moved by grace, strive by their deeds to do His will as it is known to them through the dictates of conscience. Nor does divine Providence deny the help necessary for salvation to those who, without blame on their part, have not yet arrived at an explicit knowledge of God, but strive to live a good life, thanks to His grace. Whatever goodness or truth is found among them is looked upon by the Church as a preparation for the Gospel.[21]

No one can be blamed for a lack of knowledge. If one truly seeks God but knows neither Christ nor his Church, one can be granted salvation, especially if such a person seeks to do God's will under the inspiration of divine grace, which illumines one's conscience. Salvation is also extended to those who do not know God but are living an exemplary life. Then the church regards the truth and goodness present in their lives as paving the way for the Gospel. The Divine Spirit is at work in their consciences, intellectual processes, and attempts at understanding, especially as these find expression in their religious traditions, for those who have one.

We have seen the new attitude of inclusivism in the conciliar decree *Nostra Aetate*. That watershed declaration of the church recognized the presence and activity of the Holy Spirit in other traditions and so acknowledged something of supernatural and moral value in these traditions, since they were influenced by the divine Light. The decree puts it in a welcoming kind of openness:

> The Catholic Church rejects nothing of what is true and holy in these religions. She has a high regard for the manner of life and conduct, the precepts and doctrines, which although differing in many ways from Her own teaching, nevertheless often reflect a ray of that truth which enlightens all men [persons]. Yet it proclaims and is duty bound to proclaim without fail, Christ who is "the way, the truth and the life" (John 1:6). In him, in whom God reconciled all things to himself (cf. 2 Co. 5:18–19), men [all persons] find the fullness of their religious life. . . . Let Christians, while witnessing to their own faith and way of life, acknowledge, preserve and encourage the spiritual and moral truths found among non-Christians, also their social life and culture.[22]

This statement announces the change really from an exclusivist to an inclusivist, or more accepting, perspective. It requires the faithful to recognize, protect, and promote the moral, spiritual, social, and cultural values found in these other systems of faith. Moreover, though it strongly urges this course in Christians, it declares that they must embrace this way while remaining ever faithful to the Gospel and the Christian experience. The underpinning theological insight here is the truth of the Christian faith—that these other religions, in the long run, are only preparing the way for the realization of Christ in their cultures.

In his encyclical *Dominum et Vivificantem*, John Paul II picks up on the inclusivist theme and, drawing on *Lumen Gentium* and *Gaudium et Spes*, comments on the presence and activity of the Holy Spirit in the other religions. He speaks about God's eternal and universal "plan of salvation." It should be mentioned that this pontiff has contributed more than any other in the development of the church's understanding of this eternal plan of salvation at work in the non-Christian religions. Referring to the presence and action of the Holy Spirit at all times and places in these other traditions, the pope observes:

> *We need to go further back*, to embrace the whole action of the Holy Spirit even before Christ—*from the beginning*, throughout the world, and especially in the economy of the Old Covenant. For this action

has been exercised, in every place and at every time, indeed in every individual, according to the eternal plan of salvation, whereby this action was to be closely linked with the mystery of the Incarnation and Redemption, which in its turn exercised its influence on those who believed in the future coming of Christ. . . . The Second Vatican Council, centered primarily on the theme of the Church, reminds us of the Holy Spirit's activity also "outside" the visible body of the Church. The Council speaks precisely of "all people of good will in whose hearts grace works in an unseen way." For since Christ died for all, and since the ultimate vocation of man is in fact one and divine, we ought to believe that the Holy Spirit in a manner known only to God offers to every man [person] the possibility of being associated with this paschal mystery. (*Gaudium et Spes* 22, and *Lumen Gentium* 16)[23]

This pope is concerned with the whole of humanity in its rich diversity, and instead of alienating it with the harsh rhetoric of previous ages, the church is opening its arms wide to the members of the other religions. It discerns the Divine Spirit's presence in every tradition and in every religion. These religions, in some mysterious way, are part of the divine plan of salvation for all of humankind and in every age. We saw earlier this doctrine in various papal and other ecclesial documents, especially in *Dominus Iesus*.

Rahner, during and after the council, speaking within this context, expressed the theological insight that each person must be given the opportunity to enter into and develop a genuine relationship with God. He was certain that an interior relationship with God, in the life of each individual, in these other traditions, was not sufficient, that it had to also be expressed through the person's relationships and through the available sacred institutions and other social organizations. Because we humans are social by nature, we need institutions to activate our many human capacities that flower with others. Rahner was deeply convinced that God's offer or gift of salvation has a social character to it. This social character depends on social institutions, and he realized that religion was the primary one through which God's offer of the possibility of salvation arises. The Divine touches all of us, regardless of the tradition in question, through religion. God is profoundly active in all of these religions, and his plan of salvation is operative.[24]

These other religions are places of encounter with God's grace, but once a person has made contact in a genuinely existential way with the message of the Gospel through the church's proclamation of it, these other religions, for the persons involved in the contact with the Gospel, become an illegitimate means of salvation for them.[25] They are invited by their experience and realization to move on into the church itself. Thus, inclusivism is not an absolute place of theological optimism regarding salvation for non-Christian but a way station on the way to faith in Christ.

Inclusivism more specifically entails the fulfillment doctrine; that is, the religions—though they contain, express, and transmit spiritual truths, moral values, and psychological and other human insights—are not complete without Christ and the Trinitarian focus. These other religions in which the Holy Spirit is present, spreading the invitation to salvation, find their fulfillment in the Catholic Church, which possesses the sufficient means for salvation, according to the teaching of the church and its self-understanding. It is only in the Catholic Church, and more broadly in Christianity, that we can have any degree of certitude about salvation, since the church's nature is bound up with being a carrier of salvation, and this is its primary mission.

PLURALISM: THE RELIGIONS ON AN EQUAL FOOTING

The third position, that of pluralism, has never been the view of the Magisterium, and various documents have harshly criticized this approach. The church is not willing to cross this Rubicon with all the consequences that act would set in motion. For one thing, from the perspective of the Magisterium, pluralism negates the primacy of the church as the vehicle of salvation and would relegate it to just one religion among all the others. It disregards the absolute place of the Christian understanding of revelation centered on the uniqueness of Christ and would lessen the church's evangelical mandate to proclaim the Gospel to all nations. In the remaining part of this chapter, I want to offer some insights on pluralism by way of a definition and then some criticism from the official church position and theologians.

Pluralism is a genuinely open and accepting view of the other traditions without any notion of converting them to the Christian faith. It embraces the other as other, not as an opportunity for evangelization. It does not see the other's faith as less than that of the Christian's, but perhaps on a par with Christianity. It is an attitude of real curiosity about the faith of others and a desire to learn from them the unique angle of vision on the Absolute their tradition has. Pluralism is an enthusiastic recognition that we live in an irreducibly diverse world, that plurality of faiths is an inescapable fact of life, a desirable, valuable, and precious reality of the human condition. Just as the church is keenly aware that the divine plan of salvation is at work in all this religious and spiritual diversity, might it not eventually realize that all these traditions have a mystical, theological, and metaphysical legitimacy in their own right, and not simply as preparations for the Gospel? They are, in their own way, inspired and revelations of the Absolute.

The spirit of pluralism, with its richness and multiform revelational content, is conveyed by Brian Hebblethwaite in a book entitled *Christianity and Other Religions: Selected Readings*. He says in a very challenging way to Christians:

> Christians must cease to think of their faith as bearing witness to God's final and absolute self-revelation to man. Rather, they must learn to recognize their experiences of God in Christ to be but one of many different saving encounters with the divine which have been given to different historical and cultural segments of mankind.[26]

Pluralism is the conviction that the Divine Reality, God or the Holy Spirit, is always revealing more and more of itself in the various religions of the world, and Hebblethwaite urges Christians to see beyond their truth claims that have the effect of minimizing all other traditions, reducing them to the Christian revelation or, shall we say, subordinating them to this tradition. Instead, Hebblethwaite advocates the view of the multiform nature of revelation, that the Divine is manifesting itself everywhere.

Paul Knitter, one of the leading pluralist theologians of our times, considers other religions just as valuable as Christianity. Here is his vision of pluralism:

> Other religions *may be* just as effective and successful in bringing their followers to truth, and peace, and well-being with God as Christianity has been for Christians; . . . these other religions, again because they are so different from Christianity, may have just as important a message and vision for all peoples as Christianity does. . . . Only if Christians are truly open to the Possibility . . . that there *are* many true, saving religions and that Christianity is one among the ways in which God has touched and transformed our world, only then can authentic dialogue take place.[27]

It is clear from this statement that Knitter interprets pluralism to mean that many systems of revelation exist around the world and that these systems are all valid. Pluralism does not maintain the dominance of any one of these revelational traditions but holds that these faith communities (i.e., the Hindu, Buddhist, Jewish, Jain, Taoist, Islamic, and Christian) are all of an equal status in relation to truth and value. Pluralism thus is predicated on the conviction of an ontological equality among the religions as systems of revelation—that is, as manifestations of divine disclosure or activity.

John Hick, another important pioneering pluralistic theologian, suggests a kind of disorientation for Christians as some leave behind the inclusivist claim and embrace pluralism. Although inclusivism acknowledged the extension of salvation's possibility to all persons regardless of their tradition due to the mysterious presence and action of Christ, there was still a clear understanding that the Christian faith was the only true one, in the fullest sense, but that conviction gives way when pluralism is held. Hick maintains, "[T]he move from Christian inclusivism to pluralism, although in one way seemingly so natural and inevitable, sets Christianity in a new and to some an alarming light in which there can no longer be any a priori assumption of overall superiority."[28]

Christianity had grown accustomed to being in a dominant position, and the notion of its superiority, as the ultimate revelation of the Divine in Christ, was taken for granted, but with greater knowledge of the other traditions, it becomes clear that a similar depth of revelation has occurred in the other faith traditions. As we plunge into greater relationship with the other traditions, Hick holds, we become aware that Christianity is not the focal point of revelation but God; everything revolves around this Divine One. He comments, "We have to realize that the universe of faiths centres upon God, and not upon Christianity or upon any other religion. [God] is the sun, the originative source of light and life, whom all the religions reflect in their own different ways."[29] The pluralist position is precisely the acceptance of the pluriform nature of revelation. The Divine Reality, the Absolute, God is this extraordinary eternal and infinite diamond, and the religions, as genuine manifestations of its truth, are direct refractions from this one Light. Pluralism is faith in a larger understanding of revelation that honors all the authentic traditions as emanating from the Source.

Diana Eck, the guiding thinker of Harvard's Pluralism Project, speaks eloquently of the nature of the pluralist stance primarily from its social and dialogical necessity. In her book *Encountering God: A Spiritual Journey from Bozeman to Banaras*, Eck defines pluralism in the light of the need to develop and maintain relationships, and holds that this practical necessity inspires the pluralist agenda. She observes: "Pluralism is but one of several responses to diversity and to modernity. It is an interpretation of plurality, an evaluation of religious and cultural diversity. . . . It is the ability to make a home for oneself and one's neighbors in that multifaceted reality."[30] Pluralism is focused on engagement with our brothers and sisters of other traditions, an engagement that the position of exclusivism precludes, and inclusivism complicates. In this sense, pluralism is a highly practical stance in the interreligious sphere.

Pluralism is not tolerance, which is the minimal, but acceptance of the other as other and a desire for understanding. Tolerance of itself is far removed from the spirit of pluralism.[31] Eck rejects the charge of relativism that is often leveled at pluralists, and she points out that relativism does not really have a place for commitment to one's tradition, because the sands of certainty are always shifting, whereas pluralism requires commitment to a tradition, with an enthusiastic openness to the other faiths in their members before us. Pluralism is hence both open and committed simultaneously.[32] She distinguishes relativism from pluralism insofar as relativism often lacks roots in a commitment to a tradition. She comments, "Relativism for me and for many others becomes a problem when it means the lack of commitment to any particular community or faith. If everything is more or less true, I do not give my heart to anything in particular."[33]

The pluralist abandons dogmatism for dialogue, tribalism for genuine community. Pluralism is not an acceptance of everything that comes along, but a complete receptivity to the larger picture of the Divine. Eck expresses it well:

> Pluralism is not . . . the kind of radical openness to anything and everything that drains meaning from particularity. It is, however, radical openness to Truth—to God—that seeks to enlarge understanding through dialogue. Pluralism is the complex and unavoidable encounter, difficult as it might be, with the multiple religions and cultures that are the very stuff of our world, some of which may challenge the very ground on which we stand.[34]

What Eck is saying is that pluralism represents a realistic, compassionate decision to accept actively the fact and value of diversity. It is a process of creatively and honestly engaging this diversity with great expectation of mutual understanding, growth, and an evolving, tangible sense of community between Christians and members of the other world religions. Pluralism is a commitment to dialogue because it seeks the Truth, the larger picture that emerges when we take into account the experience and insights of all the religions. Embracing this dialogical path makes us vulnerable to change from what we may learn. There is a willingness to accept the challenge.

Eck goes on to clarify that pluralism is not in any way a form of syncretism or a forced creation of a new religion based on elements from various traditions, as some critics might claim. The pluralist is not interested in developing another religion but in understanding what already exists, and the pluralist respects these traditions with their differences from the Christian faith.[35] Eck is eloquent in its insistence that pluralism has its basis in the value and practice of dialogue, interreligious dialogue. In a summarizing paragraph that evaluates each of the three positions of Christianity, she emphasizes the importance pluralism attaches to interreligious conversation:

> The isolation or dogmatism of the exclusivist is not open to dialogue. The inclusivist, while open to dialogue, does not really hear the self-understanding of the other. The truth-seeking of the pluralist, however, can be built on no other foundation than the give-and-take of dialogue. There is something we must know—both about the other and about ourselves—that can be found in no other way. She also tells us that the way of interreligious dialogue makes us true and effective instruments of relationship, the primary value of pluralism. This practice of dialogue is not concerned with debate of one another's position, but with encounters that have the aim of genuine and mutual truth-seeking.[36]

One of the clear implications of pluralism is complementarity; that is, the various world religions complete one another in very meaningful ways. This is a very significant implication. Each tradition has certain strengths and certain weaknesses. When you bring the religions together, it is always the case that each tradition is incomplete in some way, while another is able to contribute to or compensate for the deficiencies in other religions, and vice versa. For example, the Jain teaching of *ahimsa*, or nonharming, could contribute this insight to Christianity, Judaism, and Islam, which together have had so many wars. The Hindu and Buddhist emphasis on meditation and interiority could teach a lot to the Western religions, while Christianity could teach Hinduism and Buddhism a great deal about social justice and the necessity to work for it.

CRITICISMS OF PLURALISM

As we saw earlier, the Magisterium has no use for the position of pluralism because it, in a very real sense, neutralizes the claim to the primacy of truth or the absoluteness of the Catholic Church's doctrine of the preeminence of salvation through Jesus Christ through the vehicle of the church itself. In a sense, it also nullifies the church's mandate from Christ to proclaim the Gospel, since the revelation of the Incarnate Word is not seen as ultimate. This is the official church's fear. In a very powerful and perspective-generating paragraph in *Dominus Iesus*, Joseph Cardinal Ratzinger, the prefect of the Congregation for the Doctrine of the Faith, articulates the church's view and its negative attitude toward pluralism and the problem of relativism:

> The Church's constant missionary proclamation is endangered today by relativistic theories which seek to justify religious pluralism, not only de facto but also de iure [or in principle]. As a consequence, it is held that certain truths have been superseded; for example, the definitive and complete character of the revelation of Jesus Christ.[37]

It lists all the major areas of Christology: the Trinity, the authority of Sacred Scripture, and the unique role of the church. The leaders of the church regard pluralistic thinking as a threat to these truths, the integrity and identity of the Christian community.

The German Lutheran theologian Wolfhart Pannenberg, a long-time observer of the debate between inclusivist and pluralist thinkers, evaluates the overall impact on Christian confidence and certitude of the faith from the influence of pluralism. He considers the pluralistic preoccupation of some theologians to be an indication of a possible decay of the Christian faith, at least in the lives of these thinkers. Discussing the meaning of pluralism and its implications, he writes:

> What is new is that such a situation is taken seriously within the discussions of Christian theology and is felt by many theologians to challenge the foundations of what Christian doctrine has been through the centuries. An observer from the outside might be tempted to consider this phenomenon as indicating a process of erosion of the confidence of theologians in the truth of the Christian faith. To some degree such a diagnosis is probably correct, and to that extent, the current discussion on a pluralistic theology of the world's religions may be taken as a symptom of crisis within the modern Christian mind, especially in the West.[38]

Some theologians might interpret pluralism in this way, as Pannenberg's earlier comment would indicate.

Jürgen Moltmann, a theologian of the German Reformed Church, takes issue with pluralism, especially with Knitter's version, which he regards as peculiarly American and, in its own way, quite aggressive. He believes that the whole pluralistic project is ill conceived and inconsistent. He suggests that pluralism may arise out of a diverse cultural situation, as in the United States, and he wonders whether it is universally valid. Moltmann asserts:

> A pluralistic theology of religions can be no less imperialistic than the Christian theologies of religion that Knitter wants to overcome. The verbal nature of the "dialogue" process, for instance, already gives the so-called "religions of the book" an important advantage. A relativistic theory of religion may be necessary for the United States, given its diversity. Whether American pluralism is a suitable model of the relationship that should hold between world religions should be a matter of debate rather than be assumed to be true.[39]

Moltmann has some sharp criticism here, but he raises valid questions about the validity of the pluralist approach and agenda. At the same time, he may be too harsh in his view and too suspicious of something so new in historical terms.

Ours is an age of novelty, of new approaches, models, insights, and direction, a time of great danger and great promise. Interreligious dialogue, as a vehicle for building communication among diverse populations, is a vital achievement in humankind's evolution. It is a necessary skill for the survival of the human family when that family is everywhere threatened: by war, terrorism, environmental decline, overpopulation, disease, hunger, inequity, global homelessness, the growing gap between the haves and the have-nots, and many other threats. The church needs to grow in this skill, and it must become equal in importance to its highly developed and refined diplomatic activity, its political sensibilities, and its commitment to social justice.

7

TENSIONS BETWEEN MISSION AND DIALOGUE

About ten years after the close of the Second Vatican Council, in the mid-1970s, a film called *Catholics* was released in the United States. This movie is quite fascinating and provocative and even more radical than the vision of the most progressive pluralist. Martin Sheen stars as an American priest assigned to the Vatican's PCID, and Trevor Howard plays an abbot of a Benedictine monastery on a small island off the western coast of Ireland. The two struggle to implement a heart-wrenching change.

Sheen had been sent to Ireland to persuade the abbot to enforce a Vatican decree on the Eucharist. He explains to the abbot that Rome now forbids teaching the doctrine of the real presence of Christ in the Blessed Sacrament. Howard has been a monk some forty years, or all his adult life, and he begins to experience serious doubts in his own faith. He agonizes over it. He finds himself caught between the expectations of Rome, which he must meet, and the simple faith of his community, which he wants to defend and protect. The monks had become dissidents, since they stubbornly refused to accept the Vatican's dangerous, heretical new teaching. This monastery was becoming one of the important holdouts and was quickly assuming a central role of resistance to what they regarded as a total distortion of the traditional Catholic teaching.

The astounding point about this film is its novel premise: that dialogue with the Buddhists requires soft-pedaling of cherished Catholic beliefs. The conversations with Buddhist representatives had found the belief in the real presence of Christ in the Eucharist a stumbling block to Buddhist sensibilities, and Rome sought to mollify them to preserve the dialogue and, hence, the budding relationship.

Of course anyone who knows the Catholic tradition realizes that such a scenario would never, and could never, happen, but there are certainly those who fear it could. They resist interreligious dialogue and the interfaith movement, believing them to be risky enterprises for Catholics and other Christians. It would be foolish to deny that in taking the path of dialogue we are embarking on the unknown, but as Cardinal Francis Arinze, the former president of the PCID, points out, interreligious dialogue and encounter are necessary for Christianity, since Christianity itself only accounts for a third of humankind, while the rest is non-Christian, and we need to be in vital relationship with the rest of humanity.[1]

Having said this, he is keenly aware more than most that there are many risks as well. These include the possibility of losing one's faith tradition, or the real danger that faith in your tradition's beliefs might evaporate in the confusion and ambiguity of dialogue where the Christian is overwhelmed by the other's faith commitment; the danger of relativism, which greatly attempts to modify the absoluteness of Christianity's truth claims; associated with relativism, the specter of syncretism, or a forced mixing of elements from two or more traditions into an uncritical amalgam. Consider, for instance, the Christian vision wedded to transmigration in the Hindu and Buddhist views. Another danger is that a Christian may leave the church and embrace one of the other traditions. This problem is related to the loss-of-faith danger. Finally, there is the possibility of religious indifferentism. For some, too much exposure to other religions without sufficient preparation might result in a person setting aside his or her religion and all the others and simply becoming indifferent to this important part of human life.[2]

In this whole dialogical enterprise, regardless of one's tradition, it is vitally necessary to maintain a healthy sense of identity with one's own faith and particularly to be well grounded in it.[3] It is crucial to preserve one's faith identity in the midst of all the activities and demands of the interreligious encounters, whether these are actual conversations or formal exchanges, in religious worship, in comportment, in interreligious celebrations and festivals.[4] It's not good if a person loses his or her sense of identity in the midst of the often-enthusiastic presence to one another in the interfaith moment.

In this chapter, I would like to consider what appears to some as a contradiction: the mandate of the Catholic Church to proclaim the Gospel, or what is referred to as mission, and the church's other commitment to pursue a more or less open-ended dialogue with the other traditions. The church's oft-stated position on these two firmly held values, its conception of their relationship, will be reiterated here. Before presenting other views of dialogue that are somewhat critical of the Magisterium's, I would like to briefly take up the possibility of revelation in the non-Christian traditions. We will then move on to present the views of Bede Griffiths, Paul Knitter, and Raimon Panikkar on this and related issues involving pluralism. We will also more practically present some criticisms of the Vatican's *Some Aspects of Christian Meditation* and the more recent *Dominus Iesus*.

REITERATION OF THE CATHOLIC CHURCH'S VIEW

The Catholic Church, in the official teaching of the Magisterium, makes it abundantly clear that it is committed to both evangelization through the tireless proclamation of the Gospel and interreligious dialogue, the pursuance of relationships with all the other traditions around the world. Dialogue, however, is regarded as related directly to the work of the church's evangelizing mission, that clearly interreligious dialogue serves the ultimate purpose of the church of spreading the knowledge of salvation in Jesus Christ through the instrumentality of the church and its mediating role. Pope John Paul II's encyclical *Redemptoris Missio*, again with eloquent simplicity, expresses the church's understanding of the nature and role of dialogue. The pontiff writes, "Interreligious dialogue is a part of the Church's evangelizing mission. Understood as a method and means of mutual knowledge and enrichment, dialogue is not in opposition to the mission *ad gentes* [to the nations]; indeed, it has special links with that mission and is one of its expressions."[5] The church highly values dialogue and has a profound knowledge of its nature, purposes, and types, but its focus is always from the perspective of its mission to proclaim the Gospel, while interreligious dialogue presents a unique type of opportunity and audience.

Even though this is the church's understanding, commitment, and firm practice, there is a rejection of any attempts to force conversion on anyone. The pope is totally opposed to coercion in these matters and has always defended religious liberty and freedom of conscience. For example, in Sri Lanka, in an address to religious and spiritual leaders there on January 21, 1995, John Paul forcefully stated:

> Especially since the Second Vatican Council, the Catholic Church has been fully committed to *pursuing the path of dialogue and cooperating with members of other religions*. Interreligious dialogue is a precious means by which the followers of various religions discover shared

points of contact in the spiritual life, while acknowledging the differences which exist among them. The Church respects the freedom of individuals to seek the truth and to embrace it according to the dictates of conscience. In this light it firmly rejects proselytism and the use of unethical means to gain conversions.[6]

Here, we have a wonderful instance of the pope's expansive view of dialogue that approximates the expectations of the other religions in terms of what they desire from such encounters. The various traditions engaging in conversations with Christians and members of other faiths, through their representatives, regard it as an open process with no hidden agendas. The general view of the practice of dialogue is that it is a form of direct communication between or among members of the various traditions in which they share their faiths and the spiritual practices they follow.

Cardinal Arinze, who shepherded the PCID's *Dialogue and Proclamation*, an important teaching document of the Vatican in which we find the very narrow interpretation of interreligious dialogue subordinated to evangelization, also appreciates the more general view, though he is deeply committed to the church's teaching. On this general approach, he comments:

> Interreligious dialogue is a meeting of people of differing religions, in an atmosphere of freedom and openness, in order to listen to the other, to try to understand the other's religion, and hopefully to seek possibilities of collaboration. It is hoped that the other partner will reciprocate, because dialogue should be marked by a two-way and not a one-way movement. Reciprocity is in the nature of dialogue. There is a give and take. Dialogue implies both receptivity and active communication.[7]

In this generous descriptive statement, Cardinal Arinze is being gracious and open, repeating what is the basic assumption of the path of dialogue in the practice of the religions: open conversations across traditions without hidden agendas, sharing their faith and their friendship. Dialogue should have no other aim than to facilitate in-depth discussions and to draw people into collaborations for the welfare of society and the world. This is a view of interreligious dialogue that Buddhists, Hindus, Jews, Muslims, and members of indigenous traditions would find comfortable and would greatly appreciate. It has the spacious quality of friends conversing in a relaxed manner, enjoying one another's company.

At the same time, Cardinal Arinze is an official of the Holy See, and so part of the Magisterium, and he is certainly a primary defender of the church's commitment to mission and its special relationship to dialogue. In all of this, he is aware of the seeming contradiction between mission and interreligious dialogue (I say *seeming,* because from the church's perspective, there is no contradiction at all), since he raises a question that many have. He mentions how many people ask "whether dialogue and propagation of one's religion can coexist, and if so, what relationship can be established between them."[8] The church, in its Magisterium, has surely worked out the theological, practical, and policy understanding of the relationship between evangelization or proclamation and dialogue.

I believe it is true to say that the more mature we become in our in our own faith and spiritual lives, the freer we become within, the less we feel threatened by these other religions. Through study and contemplative experience, dialogue and deep encounter, we become aware of the reality of revelation in these other traditions. John Paul and other church leaders have often spoken of the dialogue of salvation and the presence of God in the non-Christian faiths. Dialogue then becomes a significant means for the church to increase its awareness of the process of salvation at work in these traditions.

REVELATION IN NON-CHRISTIAN RELIGIONS

Since there is a salvific core operative in the heart of these traditions, mysteriously guiding them to their ultimate fulfillment in Christ, according to the church's self-understanding, it is not difficult to conceive these other religions as carriers of genuine revelation, like the traditions of the Book or Judaism, Christianity, and Islam. In his seminal essay "Epiphanies of Revelation," José Pereira uncovers the existence of a stream of primitive revelation in the Asian faiths, Islam, and the indigenous traditions. In his pithy summarizing statement of this important article—something that can focus our attention on what is to follow—he writes, "Catholic thought today is moving irreversibly towards the sifting and authentication of non-Christian insights which the Church may eventually assure us are of divine origin."[9] What this means is that eventually, after considerable theological investigation, historical study, and comparative reflection, church authorities, at some point, might conclude that there is far more in these religions that are genuinely inspired by God and not merely invented by human artifice.

What is being suggested here goes beyond *Nostra Aetate,* which gives recognition to truth and moral values in the non-Christian traditions, and even surpasses the theological innovation of John Paul in his observations about the work of salvation going on in the other religions. This insight goes much further; it implies that these traditions are systems of revelation in their own right, often augmenting the revelation found in the Bible, especially the New Testament. It is true, from the perspective of the Christian faith, that these revelations, though inspired, lack a sense of finality, since they are ultimately leading up to a culmination in the Incarnate Logos, Jesus Christ. We may find, however, that we might even get some surprises, discovering that these are parallel revelations and that God is accomplishing something else in them. It's still unclear and still early in the comparative study of revelation and mysticism. One thing is quite clear, however: The Catholic Church's understanding and view of the other traditions has come a long way, and it has acquired a healthy respect for them.

Speaking within this context and drawing on a vast understanding of the other traditions, notably the Asian faiths, especially the Hindu and Buddhist cultures, Pereira, a Catholic theologian who does comparative studies, makes a distinction between Christian revelation, and the other systems of revelation, and the whole of revelation to humankind from God found in all these traditions combined.[10] What Pereira is suggesting by this distinction is that though Christian revelation represents the fullness of God's communication to humankind in Christ, there is also the whole of revelation, which takes into account all that the Spirit has revealed from the beginning of time, in every place and through the saints, sages, and mystics of each culture combined with Christian experience.

Pereira speaks of a long history of Christian universalism, the view that other figures outside the complexus of Judeo-Christian revelation could be inspired in some of their teachings, and these inspired teachings reflected certain ideas of the Christian tradition. The founders of Christian universalism were Justin (d. 165) and Clement of Alexandria (150–215).[11] It was Clement who developed the notion of the existence of a primitive inspiration or revelation; more precisely, he was convinced that there was only one Revelation, which is universally present, operative, and valid, but it expresses itself in a number of earlier revelations, epiphanies, or testaments.[12]

Pereira points out that the universalist view, which is basically similar to inclusivism in our time, rests on the discovery that a number of non-Christian religions hold insights, truths, and beliefs that the Christian faith regards as supernatural in origin, such as the Divine Logos, or the Divine Mind, the Word, or Christ, the Trinity, the Incarnation, creation out of nothing, the resurrection of Jesus, the forgiveness of sin, the Last Judgment, heaven and hell, the utter necessity of love in the pursuance of salvation, God as the end or ultimate goal of our earthly sojourn, our final and lasting beatitude, and the need for grace.[13] Moreover, the fact that these insights, beliefs, and truths emerge in non-Christian religions without any influence from Judaism, but rather are spontaneous in their provenance, suggests that they have been inspired by God.[14]

Pereira observes that it is Nicholas of Cusa (1401–1464) who is the first real universalist to formulate a theology of the religions, particularly in relationship to the Christian faith.[15] Nicholas of Cusa, or Cusanus, as he is often called, was a curial cardinal in the hierarchy of the Catholic Church. He espoused what he called the harmony, or concordance of the religions (*concordantia religionis*).[16] He sought a peaceful path to religious peace between his rich Catholic community and the followers of the Prophet Mohammed. Cusanus's *De Pace Fidei* aimed at discovering common ground and hence reconciliation, with Islam.

He was a figure who was way ahead of his time. His universalism was in service to building a peaceful relationship with Islam by emphasizing what the Christian and Islamic traditions share in common, and so what may be considered their shared revelational origin. For one thing, Cusanus was probably convinced that all such common truths between the two traditions (that is, the one God and Creator, grace, the destiny of humankind to eternal happiness, the Last Judgment, the moral life, prayer, good works, holiness, etc.) are intrinsically Catholic.[17] This cardinal's depth of theological insight has greatly advanced the church's understanding of the Holy Spirit's presence and action in other traditions and, in this instance, in the Islamic.

Pereira emphasizes the role of the church as the sole authority able to validate divine truths found in other traditions. He maintains:

> If there is but one Revelation in several epiphanies, all consummated in the epiphany of the Gospel, the authority which is the guarantor of this epiphany can also guarantee the truth of preceding epiphanies, where this has not been done before. . . . If through so doing we are enabled to glean the insights of non-Christian faiths that are of divine origin, we shall be constantly deepening our knowledge of Revelation, constantly bringing it to completion, through the infallible aid of the authority [of the Church].[18]

The Catholic Church, in its Magisterium, which guards the Revelation of the Gospel, can discern and affirm the existence of earlier manifestations of revelation; this activity increases and completes our understanding of Revelation in its total reality and truth.

It was the great theologian and original thinker, John Henry Cardinal Newman (1801–1890), whose genius and subtlety of mind have significantly advanced the Catholic Church's self-understanding in relation to other systems of faith and revelation. His clarity of thought has deepened our understanding of the activity of revelation in all the other traditions. He has had a profound impact on many theologians before and after Vatican II, and his influence on the council in the area of non-Christian religions has been impressive.

Cardinal Newman drew a very clear distinction between what he called *direct* and *indirect* revelation. Christian revelation is of the direct kind, while the pagan non-Christian faiths are of the latter. It is only Christian revelation that is free of corruption and is essentially incorruptible in the future; it is also guaranteed by the church's infallible authority. Only in the Catholic tradition is revelation guaranteed, and this precisely because of its infallibility. Cardinal Newman declares, "There is nothing impossible in the notion of a revelation occurring without evidence that it is a revelation. . . . But Christianity is not of this nature: it is a revelation which comes to us as a revelation, as a whole, objectively, and with a profession of infallibility."[19]

Cardinal Newman was certain that revelation required an authority to recognize it, and only under this condition was it possible: "A revelation is not given, if there be not authority to decide what it is that is given."[20] Without such an authority, we cannot be certain what is directly inspired by God and what is not, or what is indirect, and perhaps corrupted, or corruptible in the future.

The Catholic Church, and Christianity more generally, is faced with the immense task of encountering and evaluating the inspired truths of these other traditions in the light of the fullness of revelation of the Incarnate Son. As Pereira concludes:

> Catholic thought, since Vatican II's *Declaration on the Relationship of the Church to Non-Christian Religions*, is moving irreversibly in the direction of the sifting and authentication of non-Christian insights. . . . [T]he Church will essentially see its way to assuring us of their divine origin. If that happens, we shall be able to contemplate in wonder the one Revelation unfolded in a sequence of epiphanies.[21]

We can already notice this kind of movement in the thinking and evaluation of the teaching church, the Magisterium, in its insistence on the operating of the divine plan of salvation in all the religions, especially the ancient ones. Notice, also, in the foregoing discussion of Christian universalism, that it is not an argument for pluralism, but more of an inclusivist view with which the Magisterium would no doubt feel comfortable.

MORE RECENT VIEWS

It is very common for Christians to encounter other faiths in various contexts and to learn deeply from these experiences, to develop a genuine respect for these faiths, their spiritual, moral, psychological, and even theological authenticity. Some of these various contexts include study, actual dialogical opportunities, missionary situations, mystical realizations from contact with the ultimate teaching of the traditions, special breakthroughs in contemplation, or the saintly example of representatives of these other traditions. All of these Christians are loyal to Christ—indeed, have a depth of faith—but they are not willing to impose their faith on their interlocutors, whether Hindu, Buddhist, Jewish, Jain, Muslim, or otherwise. Persons who have had this type of awakening to interreligious sensitivity from contact with non-Christian forms of revelation, or spiritual experience, cease to be inclusivists and embrace some form of pluralism.

BEDE GRIFFITHS

Such was the case with Bede Griffiths, who was inspired by the truth in the other traditions. He often discoursed about complementarity, how the religions complete one another's deficiencies, in personal conversations, homilies, letters, books, articles, interviews, and dialogues with members of other faiths. I remember hearing him address this issue many times in the twenty years I knew him. Bede's contribution on this matter was more on the level of spirituality and cross-cultural mysticism, rather than in an academic context. His insistence on openness in dialogue, and respecting the right of the other to his or her inner experience, not wanting to change the other through conversion, was equaled by his absolute commitment to Christ in his own faith.

PAUL KNITTER

Pluralist thinkers, philosophers, theologians, and spiritual writers abound, such as John Hick, Langdon Gilkey, Stanley Samartha, Raimon Panikkar, Rosemary Radford Ruether, Marjorie Hewitt Suchoki, and Aloysius Pieris, to name a few, but one of the great leaders of pluralism, who writes with clarity, subtlety, and a comprehensive sensitivity, is Paul Knitter. The Vatican has been very disturbed by his writings and regards them as exposing the church's teaching to the dangers of relativism. His pluralism is threatening to the Magisterium, and it does not accept his approach.

Knitter has searched for a common point to relate the religions in dialogue. Although he is himself a theocentrist, intuiting and believing that God is the foundation of everything, he does not feel this conviction can serve as the basis for interreligious dialogue. Similarly, though he appreciates mysticism, spirituality, and contemplation, he doesn't argue for a mystical center as the common ground in interreligious conversation. Nor is he persuaded that a common essence or a universal faith dimension is the foundation of dialogue, even though he is open to these realities. What is needed is an approach that really honors the faith of the participants. He explains this fundamental point:

> Theologians who argue that Christianity needs a new way of relating to other religions are trying to promote an interreligious dialogue that will be genuinely *pluralistic*—one that will avoid preestablished absolutist or definitive positions in order to allow that all the participants have an equally valid voice and that each participant can really hear, as much as possible, what the other is saying.[22]

He is very suspicious of both exclusivism and inclusivism in the Christian tradition, and he is eloquent in his insight that the maxim *extra ecclesiam nulla salus* is actually a means of social and even political control of others, our non-Christian friends. He is convinced that exclusivism, along with inclusivism, is very harmful, because both these models of relationship with the church and salvation depend on exploiting and subordinating the various religions and cultures of the world to the church. Neither of them are able to listen to the other in the way in which the other experiences that he or she has really been heard as other, rather than in a polite sense that waits for the opportunity to evangelize this other. He thus sets aside both exclusivism and inclusivism.[23]

In a meaningful passage at the end of his book *No Other Name*, Knitter identifies the real purpose of dialogue. Although he is committed to Christ and to his uniqueness vis-à-vis the other religions, his is a gentle approach. He locates the purpose of dialogue in the value and necessity of communication itself, especially in relation to the critical issues of the world and notably the urgent problem of the poor and oppressed. Referring to this purpose, he says:

> Whether the question of Jesus' uniqueness is answered, whether Jesus does or does not prove to be final and normative, is not, really, the central or primary purpose of dialogue. The task at hand, demanded of Christianity and all religions by both the religious and the sociopolitical world in which they live, is that the religions speak and listen to each other, that they grow with and from each other, that they combine efforts for the welfare, the salvation, of all humanity.[24]

The mutual responsibility all the participants in interreligious dialogue have is to the whole world and to one another. He considers dialogue as a sacred responsibility that carries us beyond our narrow interests. Therefore, he is convinced the Magisterium's position is too one-sided and not conducive to deep listening in practice, since there's always an ulterior motive.

When it comes to the praxis dimension of interreligious conversation—that is, the actual existential encounters, the discussions that take place, and what should ground them—Knitter is passionately committed to a social justice focus. The debate on this issue has centered around the question of what the common ground is or should be, or even whether a common ground is possible in the sphere of interfaith encounter, whether this common ground is God, the Spirit, infinite consciousness, the mystical center, or something else. Knitter suggests a more practical common ground that draws from the universal human experience. He sees this shared concern of the religions in the struggle for justice:

> Within the struggle for liberation and justice with and for the many different groups of oppressed persons, believers from different traditions can experience together, and yet differently, that which grounds their resolves, inspires their hopes, and guides their actions to overcome injustice and to promote unity. . . . Perhaps better than the monastery or the mystic's mountain, the struggle for justice can become the arena where Hindus and Muslims, Buddhists and Christians and Jews, can sense, and begin to speak about, that which unites them.[25]

What is so inspiring about this proposal is that it has come out of Knitter's consistent commitment to the poor, oppressed, and marginalized people of the world. I believe his approach makes a lot of sense with the caveat that we must also keep before us our own religious identity, which of course informs our concern for justice, peace, and ecological responsibility.

RAIMON PANIKKAR

Raimon Panikkar is one of the most extraordinary cross-cultural thinkers on the planet and is, in his own life, a marriage of East and West. His father was a Hindu, a Brahmin from Kerela in South India, while his mother was a Spanish Catholic from the Barcelona area. Surely this background has had an impact on the development of his thought and the creativity, originality, and depth of his contribution. His thought is subtle, stretching language to sensitively include the other traditions from within, understanding them in their own right, and experiencing them from within a Christian theological perspective. Panikkar is perhaps the most literate comparative theologian to appear to date. His theological language and his contemplative awareness have greatly served his understanding.

Panikkar characterizes the nature of interreligious dialogue, the relating of the religions in encounter and conversation, as one that enriches, deepens, and expands one another's understanding and life. He says that a mature relationship of the traditions in the dialogical situation "is not one of assimilation, or of substitution (the latter under the misnomer of 'conversion'), but one of *mutual fecundation*."[26] The emphasis is on a kind of communion of insight that draws on one another's tradition, and a shedding of light from one tradition on another, and vice versa, in such a way that the participants understand their core truths and experiences in a new way—hence the experience of mutual fecundation. Panikkar's aim in interreligious conversation is to uncover a depth of continuity between and among the religions, which must exist given the one ultimate divine Mystery to which all the religions relate themselves and in which they are nourished and sustained.[27]

It is clear he does not accept the inclusivist position articulated in the Magisterium's teaching, since this approach seems to reduce the faith of the other and does not converse without an agenda that is governed by the essential goal and norm of the church's evangelizing mission. Panikkar can only respect his interlocutors and relate to them in their own terms from the perspective of an inner contemplative, linguistic, and theological spaciousness that makes room for the other. At the same time, he does so as a Christian, and he regards the Christian experience of and reflection on the Trinity as the metaphysical and mystical junction where the religions can meet and be understood by the Christian. He is not saying that the Trinity is the common ground of the religions in dialogue but the matrix for Christians in their attempts to understand the divine Mystery experienced and formulated in the other faiths.[28]

REFLECTION ON
SOME ASPECTS OF CHRISTIAN MEDITATION

Here I want to briefly consider some reservations about the document of the Vatican's Congregation for the Doctrine of the Faith, *Some Aspects of Christian Meditation*. The reservations arise out of the church's contemplative/mystical tradition and will rely on conversations I've had with Bede Griffiths and Thomas Keating as well as my own processing of the document.

This statement arose in a cultural climate of interspirituality, the greater willingness to explore the mystical practices of other traditions, especially those of the Hindu, Buddhist, Sufi, and Jewish schools of spiritual life. As a significant minority of Christians have been imbibing meditative disciplines, yoga, and studying the doctrines of the East and elsewhere, the Vatican has become concerned that such Catholics are risking the loss of their Christian identity. This teaching document emphasizes that all such prayer has to be Christ-centric. *Some Aspects of Christian Meditation* is perfectly consistent with the church's understanding of its mandate to proclaim the Gospel and to guard the sense of Christian identity focused on Christ. As a statement of theological principle, it is understandable, but it needs more development in terms of the church's very subtle and valuable contemplative tradition.

Bede Griffiths often talked about this document in public discourses and personal conversations. He felt that the declaration was much too Eurocentric and thus theologically somewhat provincial. In the light of his long experience with Hindu mysticism and its highly developed meditation practice, its extraordinarily deep psychological experience, its pervasive understanding of the Divine Reality, informed and deepened by his own Christian contemplation, Bede interpreted this statement coming from the CDF as weak and ignorant of the spiritual depths of the other traditions.

Thomas Keating, the great spiritual teacher in the Catholic tradition, had similar reservations, regarding the document as essentially unfinished for many of the same reasons. He would add that more could have been said from Christian mysticism and the monastic experience to challenge this undeveloped state of the teaching from the CDF. All of us have discerned that the persons who worked on *Some Aspects of Christian Meditation* were not themselves mystics or contemplatives, and they certainly had very little understanding of the spiritualities of the other traditions, both of which are necessary to create a balanced document.

I want to offer an incident in my spiritual life that illustrates the limitations of the CDF declaration on prayer or meditation. Recently, I had some extra time for prayer, and I decided to do an additional contemplative meditation before going to bed. It had been a very long day, and I sat in my chair at 12:20 A.M. for what I thought would be ten minutes. Two hours later I came back to ordinary consciousness. I don't know where I was. I wasn't asleep. I was in a state of total absorption in the Divine, but I didn't know it because I wasn't aware of myself. It reminds me of an old saying of the Desert tradition: "If you know you are praying, then you aren't really praying." Now, the CDF document on meditation emphasizes the Christ-centric focus in prayer and meditation. Every Christian mystic knows that it is not always possible to center attention on Christ, and this teaching of the Vatican hasn't taken this fact into consideration.

SOME COMMENTS ON *DOMINUS IESUS*

It is well known that CDF's promulgation of the document *Dominus Iesus* occasioned considerable controversy around the world, and it has greatly complicated the church's relations with non-Christian faiths, as well as with other Christian communions. It has stirred anger, resentment, sorrow, and deep anguish in our non-Christian friends and has proven to be an obstacle to genuine dialogue. The tone, direction, spirit, and perceived insensitivity of the declaration caught many off guard, and it has really damaged relations between the Catholic Church and the other world religions. As I pointed out earlier, I was amazed at the theological clarity of the document in presenting the teaching of the Magisterium and the wider Catholic tradition. I wonder, though, since the tragic occurrence of September 11, 2001, whether this event has an implication for presenting these kinds of documents in the future. What I'm suggesting is that *Dominus Iesus* is a highly inflammatory statement, one that could potentially spark grave conflicts. I think the promulgation of the document at this juncture in history was probably a mistake.

The Catholic Theological Society of America sponsored a panel discussion on it at its annual conference in June 2001 in Milwaukee and published its proceedings. I want to refer to one of the active participants in this important event, Francis X. Clooney, a Jesuit theologian who teaches at Boston College. While Father Clooney's remarks were scholarly, polite, and somewhat diplomatic, he did make a remark that cautions the Catholic Church about its language and the need to give a good example:

> *Dominus Iesus* proclaims its truths in a global context where many people of different traditions are listening and determined to participate, where we entirely control neither the vocabulary nor the interpretation of what we say, and where even the most authoritative Catholic teachers must provide publicly accessible evidence for the claims they make, if they wish to be taken seriously. This wider theological conversation about the truth of the lordship of Jesus requires a more nuanced teaching process than has previously been customary; to teach the truth of our faith in the new millennium we must teach differently, in dialogue and receptive to the suggestions and critiques of persons inside and outside the Church.[29]

John Pawlikowski, a Catholic leader in the dialogue with Judaism and a professor of Social Ethics at Catholic Theological Union in Chicago, is more blunt in his criticism of the declaration. He refers to the offensive tone of the document, how it is so insensitive to the personal, existential context of so many interreligious conversations. He regards *Dominus Iesus* as essentially unconscious of this personal level of engagement. He observes:

> Dialogue is very much a personal encounter of believers. I could not speak some of the language of *Dominus Iesus* to my dialogue partners. Nor could the Catholic monks in the intermonastic dialogue who have lived and prayed together for months at a time speak those words. *Dominus Iesus* remains totally oblivious to the personal side of the dialogue. While dialogue cannot be based totally on personal experience, it cannot remain exclusively on the "objective" level as *Dominus Iesus* does.[30]

The Catholic Church has to listen as much as it speaks; otherwise dialogue will become impossible or very difficult. *Dominus Iesus* seems to contradict the spirit of Vatican II and the examples of John XXIII, Paul VI, and John Paul II himself. It doesn't appear to be coming from a very real place of listening but rather represents a kind of spiritual imperialism that cannot accept or live with the possibility of any rivals. The cure for this kind of attitude is sincere, vulnerable dialogue without sacrificing the nature of the church and the contribution it makes.

8

INTERRELIGIOUS ENCOUNTER AND DIALOGUE

The Existential Reality

In the 1990s, in the intermonastic hospitality program, an ongoing exchange between North American Benedictine and Cistercian monks and nuns, under the umbrella of Monastic Interreligious Dialogue, and Tibetan Buddhist monks and nuns in India, under the authority of the Central Administration of the Dalai Lama's government-in-exile, a small group of Tibetan monastics stayed at Osage Monastery in Sand Springs, Oklahoma, with a Benedictine community of nuns. During their visit, the nuns organized a public event for the Tibetans and invited people to meet them for an evening event. Everything went well until an evangelical minister asked a provocative question. He blurted out to the Tibetans, "Do you know Jesus Christ?" Of course they were taken aback by the challenging tone and force of this man's question. They were not certain what he was really asking and consulted among themselves. Then one of them turned to the man and said very politely and kindly, "We haven't met Jesus Christ, but we know many of his followers, and we like them very, very much!" The whole audience roared with laughter and clapped enthusiastically.

This incident illustrates the importance of the human dimension in interreligious experience. It is a very central factor that must never be neglected in any characterization of the actual situation of dialogue. What this story reveals is the sensitivity of the Tibetans in a tense encounter with an unprepared and insensitive Christian who was not very kind to these Buddhists. The Dalai Lama often remarks that genuine and meaningful dialogue is only possible between friends, and when it comes to dialogue of a substantive nature that's been going on for a while, this quality is clearly the case. I have certainly witnessed this phenomenon in my own life in encounters with Hindus, Buddhists, Jews, and Muslims.

115

In the living reality and dynamics of interreligious conversation, miraculous breakthroughs can happen, and often they are simply the result of basic human kindness and real presence to one another. A dramatic example of this is an encounter that occurred between Rami Shapiro, a Jewish mystical teacher, and a Palestinian student during an interfaith event at the start of the Iraqi war. The Palestinian student approached Rami at a break in the program and asked whether he could speak with him. The young man was quite distraught and angry. He broke down in Rami's presence, violently shouting, "I don't know what to do. I feel like going to Iraq, strap explosives on my body, and blow up Americans! What should I do?" Rabbi Shapiro looked at him with tender understanding and compassion and said calmly, "Rather than blow yourself up and hide in death, why don't you wake up to love!" The Palestinian youth took in this challenge and responded that he'd give it some thought, but clearly he wasn't expecting this kind of response from Rami. At the end of the conference, the Palestinian student sought Rami out again and remarked, "I think I understand what you are telling me." Such encounters happen all the time, but they illustrate the miracles of grace that frequently occur in the interreligious arena.

In this chapter, we will consider in some depth the more subtle dialogue between monastics in the Catholic and Buddhist traditions, beginning with Thomas Merton's historic visit to Dharamsala in 1968, during his fateful pilgrimage to Asia. We will look at the intermonastic hospitality exchange and then its evolution into a growing, substantive conversation that expressed itself in a three-hour Buddhist-Christian encounter[1] at the Parliament of the World's Religions in 1993, as we saw earlier, as well as the documents of the *Universal Declaration on Nonviolence* and the *Resolution on Tibet*, and culminating in Gethsemani I and Gethsemani II, the days of discussions and sharing at Merton's Abbey of Gethsemani, his monastery in Kentucky. We will move to briefly reflect on the Hindu-Christian dialogue preceding and following Vatican II in India.

INTERMONASTIC DIALOGUE: CATHOLIC–BUDDHIST

In June 1977, after the Petersham Conference in Petersham, Massachusetts, which brought together Christian monastics from North America and Europe with Hindu and Buddhist monastics for ten days, a group of Benedictines and Cistercians established the North American Board for East-West Dialogue, which was the result of a mandate from Rome to carry on the Catholic Church's official dialogue with monastics of the Asian traditions and other contemplatives. In the late 1980s, this organization's name was changed to Monastic Interreligious Dialogue. The outreach to Hindu and Buddhist monastics and other spiritual teachers and contemplative masters was inspired by the example of Thomas Merton, especially his conversations with the Dalai Lama[2] in Dharamsala in November 1968, and the dialogical activities of Bede Griffiths, Raimon Panikkar, Abhishiktananda, and many others in India in deep encounter with the Hindu tradition.

In 1980, the North American Board for East-West Dialogue established the Intermonastic Hospitality Program with the Tibetans, and this exchange has been going on ever since. The arrangement was that for a period of six months, four to six Tibetan monks and nuns would come to America and spend two to three weeks to a month in a Benedictine or Trappist community in the United States or Canada. When a particular visit ended in one monastery, a new one would begin elsewhere. The following year, a wave of Christian monastics would travel to India and stay for some months in Tibetan monasteries and nunneries, spending a few weeks to a month in one of these institutions and then moving on to the next one.

During these intermonastic hospitality exchanges, the monks and nuns would share in the lives of their hosts, their prayer, work, study, and conversations. Many wonderful friendships developed in these significant visits, and as time passed, more in-depth dialogues occurred. An organic evolution happened as the intermonastic hospitality exchange became an intermonastic dialogue and these dialogical exchanges became a communion of hearts and minds. Monastic Interreligious Dialogue, in consultation with the Dalai Lama and his advisers, decided to upgrade the exchange program into something more substantive: the depth of spiritual conversation becoming friendship, leading into genuine communion.

Sister Pascaline Coff, a Benedictine nun and one of the leaders of MID, at Gethsemani I in July 1996, has reflected on this transition from intermonastic hospitality exchange to intermonastic dialogue and the communion of spiritual friendship. She expresses it so succinctly:

> This point of spiritual exchange between Buddhist and Christian monastics began decades ago as "a preliminary experience in hospitality," "a prelude to in-depth dialogue," and "a mutually agreed groundbreaking first step." Over the years, this point has become, in the words of William Johnston, "Friendship, the crown of authentic dialogue."[3]

Again, this is the very same kind of insight the Dalai Lama emphasizes about interreligious dialogue—that it is really only possible when friendship is its basis. Sister Pascaline is drawing attention to the history involved, and that history illustrates the truth of the Dalai Lama's observation. When friendship develops, an intimacy, profundity, and subtlety of dialogue just happen, as we saw earlier in the example of Ignatius Hirudayam and his Hindu-Christian group in Madras, now called Chennai.

THE *UNIVERSAL DECLARATION ON NONVIOLENCE*

The friendship that characterizes this Christian-Buddhist dialogue that is becoming increasingly deeper and more intimate contributed to the emergence, formulation, and proclamation of the *Universal Declaration on Nonviolence: The Incompatibility of Religion and War.* This document was the fruit of the dialogue of the hands between Monastic Interreligious Dialogue and the Dalai Lama. It represents a kind of declaration of independence between the religions and war making, or the supporting of war and any other form of violence. Here is the declaration:

> This document is an attempt to set forth a vision of nonviolence within the context of an emerging global civilization in which all forms of violence, especially war, are totally unacceptable as means to settle disputes between and among nations, groups, and persons. This new civilization is global in scope, universal in culture, and based on love and compassion, the highest moral/spiritual principles of the various historical religions. Its universal nature acknowledges the essential fact of modern life: the interdependence of nations, cultures, and religious traditions.
>
> As members of religious groups throughout the world, we are increasingly aware of our responsibility to promote peace in our age and the ages to come. Nevertheless, we recognize that in the history of the human family, people of various religions, acting officially in the name of their respective traditions, have either initiated or collaborated in organized and systematic violence or war. These actions have at times been directed against other religious traditions, groups, and nations, as well as within particular religious traditions. This pattern of behavior is totally inappropriate for spiritual persons and communities. Therefore, as members of world religions, we declare before the human family, that:
>
> Religion can no longer be an accomplice to war, to terrorism or to any other forms of violence, organized or spontaneous, against any

member of the human family. Because this family is one, global, interrelated, our actions must be consistent with this identity. We recognize the right and duty of governments to defend the security of their people and to relieve those afflicted by exploitation and persecution. Nevertheless, we declare that religion must not permit itself to be used by any state, group or organization for the purpose of supporting aggression for nationalistic gain. We have an obligation to promote a new vision of society, one in which war has no place in resolving disputes between and among states, organizations, and religions.

In making this declaration, we the signatories commit ourselves to this new vision. We call upon all the members of our respective traditions to embrace this vision. We urge our members and all peoples to use every moral means to dissuade their governments from promoting war or terrorism. We strongly encourage the United Nations Organization to employ all available resources toward the development of peaceful methods of resolving conflicts among nations.

Our declaration is meant to promote such a new global society, one in which nonviolence is preeminent as a value in all human relations.

We offer this vision of peace, mindful of the words of Pope Paul VI to the United Nations in October 1965: "No more war; war never again!"[4]

This jointly sponsored statement expresses a certain eloquence and relevance. It has influenced the formation of other documents, notably the Parliament of the World's Religions' "Towards a Global Ethic: An Initial Declaration," which was released in the summer of 1993.[5]

Another important MID initiative was taken during the Parliament of the World's Religions in late August 1993. In the context of the Buddhist-Christian Monastic Dialogue on September 4, 1993, Monastic Interreligious Dialogue, with the knowledge and approval of His Holiness the Dalai Lama and his government, announced and promulgated at the Parliament itself, the *Resolution on Tibet*, which was also the fruit of the dialogue of the hands between Buddhist and Christian monastics. Here is this very brief but profoundly meaningful resolution:

We have observed the intense suffering of the Tibetan People that has been inflicted on them for more than four decades. It is with concern, empathy, a deep sense of responsibility and solidarity that we express our collective outrage at the brutal and callous actions of the People's Republic of China in Tibet. These actions include cultural genocide, torture, forced abortion, sterilization and systematic

violation of the human rights of the Tibetan People, as well as de-
forestation and dumping of nuclear waste in Tibet. Above all, the
massive transfer of Chinese immigrants into Tibet which has already
transformed the Tibetans into an insignificant minority in their own
country, threatens the very existence of the Tibetan national and cultural identity. Such actions are thoroughly reprehensible and morally
repugnant to all people within the religions, and even to those with
no religion.

Therefore, considering the seriousness of the situation in Tibet, we
call for the complete and immediate restoration of the legitimate
rights of the Tibetan People, and urge the international community
to address the issue of Tibet at various world forums, in particular at
the United Nations.[6]

Although MID and Christian monastics in North America have a
very substantial connection with Tibetan monastics and Tibetan Buddhism, there is a strong relationship with monks, nuns, and laity of the
Theravadan and Zen traditions of the Buddhist Dharma, and representatives of these schools of Buddhism are present at MID conferences and
retreats. The Intermonastic Hospitality Exchange and its evolution into
the Intermonastic Dialogue Exchange have been greatly aided by the
joint initiative of the *Universal Declaration on Nonviolence* and later the
unilateral action of MID in offering the *Resolution on Tibet*. These actions
have been regarded by the Tibetans as signs of what the Dalai Lama often calls universal responsibility, and they have played a role in the move
to a deeper level of dialogical explorations as seen in Gethsemani I and
Gethsemani II.

GETHSEMANI ENCOUNTER I

The first Gethsemani Encounter occurred July 22 to 27, 1996, with
forty-six participants composed of Christian and Buddhist monastics and
a number of observers. Each of the full working days of the first session
had a topical focus, including (1) The Practice of Prayer and Meditation
in the Spiritual Life, (2) The Stages in the Process of Spiritual Development, (3) The Role of the Teacher and the Community in the Spiritual
Life, and (4) The Spiritual Goals of Personal and Social Transformation.[7]
Under these four general topics, twenty-five talks were given, ten by
Christians and fifteen by Buddhists. These talks were fairly brief but were
meant to present substantial understanding of the inner workings of
Christian and Buddhist spirituality. Insights were offered and then devel-

oped in the subsequent dialogues.[8] In the dialogues themselves, numerous topics were covered: mind, anger, purity, stages, love, humility, teacher, language, Scripture, (spiritual) practice, experience, discernment, grace, suffering, sacrifice, violence, social action, tolerance, women's issues, and unity.[9] The week ended with two tributes to Thomas Merton, one by James Connor, a Trappist abbot who knew him well, and the other by the Dalai Lama.[10] There were then some final reflections given by a number of participants and observers; these appear in an epilogue in *The Gethsemani Encounter*,[11] the proceedings of the intermonastic conference.

The Buddhist and Christian monastics, along with the observer companions, explored the differences and commonalities between these two venerable and mature traditions in their contemplative experience. They shared life together for these wonderfully full days, enjoying meals, prayer, meditation, liturgy, Buddhist rituals, personal conversations, more formal dialogues, walks together, and many warm-hearted exchanges, with much laughter and the incomparable joy of evolving friendships.

Jeffrey Hopkins, who describes himself as a nonsectarian Buddhist, though a scholar and practitioner of Vajrayana, or Tibetan Buddhism, gave an informative talk entitled "Nirvana, Buddhahood and the Spiritual Life," followed by Donald Mitchell, representing Christianity, who presented a parallel lecture called "God, Creation and the Spiritual Life."[12] Both were attempting to set the stage conceptually for the dialogues to follow by giving a clear picture of the metaphysics of each tradition: for Buddhism, the notion of Nirvana, the unconditioned, eternal state reached when the mind is not clouded by selfish desires, with the whole disciplined approach to spiritual development required to attain the goal of inner liberation; for Christianity, in the realization of God as the transcendent and immanent Source of being, the universe(s), and the evolution of spiritual life that flows forth from the Divine as personal, engaged, and affirming of us and our ultimate destiny for beatitude, or Paradise, or permanent intimacy with God.

Jeffrey Hopkins points out that purification of our grasping or attachment to our personal identity is the basis of Buddhist spirituality, which allows us to experience our true Buddha-nature, the clear light of the mind, unconditioned and free, calm and pure, capable of wisdom and compassion, as well as empty of inherent existence. Developing understanding in this direction is the goal of all Buddhist practice. Hopkins elaborates:

> The clear light nature of the mind is described in certain *tantras* [Tibetan Buddhist texts] as the fundamental, innate mind of clear light.

It is fundamental in the sense that its continuum exists forever. . . . It has no beginning and no end in time. The mind of clear light is called the "all-good." It is also called the "basis of all" in that it is the basis of all phenomena, both of cyclic existence and of Nirvana. . . .

The second way of conceiving the Buddha-nature is as the absence of the inherent existence of the mind. This does not refer to the non-existence of the mind, nor does it suggest that the mind lacks definition or nature. Rather, it refers to the mind's not existing independently, under its own power. The mind is not established by way of its own character, from its own side. The emptiness of inherent existence is the true nature of all phenomena.

All beings are empty of independent existence.[13]

When we are aware of the true nature of the mind, we are free of the limiting conditions and consequences of desire and willing arising from selfish ends and ignorance. Then we are inwardly free to be compassionate and loving. Being aware of the clear light nature of the mind, its eternal and unconditioned reality, we are also aware that the mind does not and cannot exist by itself. It is, in this sense, emptiness, since it has no intrinsic separate existence unto itself. It is related to all other sentient beings. Realizing these basic truths positions us to walk the path of enlightenment in which we can work for the liberation of all sentient beings, freeing them from the cycle of rebirth, or *samsara*. Hopkins himself is convinced that Buddhism and Christianity are a lot closer than we might at first imagine, and we could easily find parallels between God and emptiness, and nirvana.[14]

Donald Mitchell goes on to unfold the Christian understanding of the ultimate ground of reality, its relation to the cosmos, nature, humanity, and our life in relation to it. This, of course, in the Christian view, as in those of Judaism, Islam, and other theistic traditions, is what we mean when we speak of God. Mitchell, wanting to clarify this essential point in relation to the dialogue with Buddhists, states, "God is the uncreated, unborn, unproduced Ground of this created and conditioned order of things."[15] He also relates this metaphysical insight to the fundamental metaphysical foundation of Buddhism in its absolute, nirvana, or its Pali equivalent, *nibbana*. Nirvana, like God or the Godhead, is the unborn, uncreated, unconditioned Source or ultimate in Buddhist philosophy. He develops the Christian understanding, really a biblical insight, of *creatio ex nihilo,* that the Divine creates out of no preexisting substance or material, but purely from its own power, creativity, and ideas. This creation is a pure gift of God to us and all beings who inhabit it and are in transit through it. The motive of creation—that is, why God creates—is to share himself with us through love. The universe is conceived and sustained in love.[16] This formulation is very much the Christian vision and draws on the ancient and medieval tradition of Christian theology, which understood that the Divine is self-diffusive of itself by its very nature and so creates from the motive of its goodness and love.

Mitchell then turns to the dynamics of spiritual development in intimacy with God and eloquently comments on how close this relationship is in its unitive and transformative character, how the relationship is a deepening likeness to the Divine. Reflecting on the nature of transformation in the Christian experience, he quotes Paul's 2 Corinthians 3:18 and then draws out his meaning in the practice of the spiritual life:

> Consider for a moment the following scripture passage that deals with Christian transformation in God: "With our unveiled faces reflecting like mirrors the brightness of the Lord, all grow brighter and brighter as we are turned into the image that we reflect; this is the work of the Lord who is Spirit." For us the term "spirit" . . . refers to the very pure and clear essence of consciousness—perhaps something similar to the "mind of clear light" as understood in the Tibetan tradition.
>
> In the above passage from scripture, the point is that the spiritual "brightness of the Lord" is a luminosity, a clarity and purity of the Holy Spirit that transforms us in mind and body into what we receive: we become what we reflect in our spiritual life. . . . By sharing in the divine life of God, we become "divinized," to use a term coined by the Fathers of our Church. Therefore, as in the advanced forms of tantric practice, we do not just worship the divine as an external deity. We become divine by sharing in that reality at the innermost core of our consciousness.[17]

Transformation has a moral, intellectual, or wisdom level and an essential, or ontological dimension; that is, the change that occurs is radically operative in all areas of our being. Our awareness is greatly expanded; our capacity for love, mercy, kindness, and compassion is enlarged; and our wisdom is informed by divine perception—all as a consequence of union with God where we more closely resemble the Divine in essential being. This bears some similarity to realizing the Buddha-nature, the clear light reality of pure mind in the Buddhist tradition.

His Holiness the Dalai Lama gave three significant talks during this historic week: "Harmony, Dialogue and Meditation," "The Path to

Calm Abiding," and "Spiritual Guidance and the Attainment of Nirvana." In "The Path to Calm Abiding," which is a form of meditation, His Holiness addresses how to develop mindfulness, so necessary for a mature meditation practice. His advice is eminently practical:

> To develop strong mindfulness, it is important to act mindfully in all aspects of one's behavior. Whether one is walking about, or one is standing, or sitting down, or even lying down, it is important to maintain mindfulness of what you are doing. In order to maintain mindfulness continuously, it is necessary to have conscientiousness. This is very important for *all* religious practitioners.[18]

All forms of meditation, or contemplation, allow this quality of concentration called mindfulness to emerge, becoming habitual, and with mindfulness, the capacity for depth of awareness and subtlety evolves.

Then in "Spiritual Guidance and the Attainment of Nirvana," the Dalai Lama remarks on the role of the spiritual teacher in attaining nirvana:

> For there to be a good and strong spiritual community, there must be teachers who teach the path well, and for that, they must provide proper role models. Teaching about spiritual matters does not just take place on the intellectual level. The teacher must also show what is taught to his or its followers by example. The teacher must provide an example for the eyes of his or its followers. Then the students will develop a genuine appreciation or respect.[19]

Here His Holiness is referring to the necessity of seeing genuine holiness of life, as the fruit of transformation, in the actual spiritual teacher, a fruit that demonstrates consistency between wisdom and character. There have been many spiritual masters who have not shown this consistency and have not truly surrendered in their hearts. The Dalai Lama is thus providing a gentle warning in his guidance on this matter.

His Holiness then goes on to consider the nature of nirvana, of which there are many opinions. His own view is that nirvana is a quality of the mind, the original nature of the mind, its deeper reality that is always present—the Buddha-nature that we all are in our intrinsic being. Nirvana is the unconditioned nature of who we are, the very inner reality of the mind as clear light, unfettered by conditioned existence, and the relative reality of our culture and society. It is the Absolute, in the Buddhist understanding, but it is not personal, as the Divine is. As the Dalai Lama expresses it, "The very basis, the foundation of Nirvana is always with us. It is not something that is sought from the outside."[20] Enlightenment is ultimately living from the awareness of the nirvanic realization.

Sister Donald Corcoran, a Benedictine nun and expert on the master–disciple relationship, gave a wonderful talk on the role of the spiritual guide from the monastic experience, and this is of course the Christian vision stemming from the early Catholic Church. One of the points she emphasizes is that the human spiritual teacher, or guide, is an instrument of the Divine's. She puts it succinctly: "It is the Spirit, promised by Jesus Christ, who will 'teach you all things.' This is the reason the Christian tradition has always emphasized that Christ or the Holy Spirit is the true guide of the soul—the human teacher being a vehicle of grace, as it were."[21]

From the inception of the Encounter, throughout its days, and beyond, the participants and the observers sensed the historical value of what they were doing together. The editors of *The Gethsemani Encounter* express it beautifully:

> There was a sense that what we were discussing—and what was happening—at Gethsemani was relevant to the destiny of all humankind. There was an awareness that even with our differences, we were experiencing a dialogical movement from, in Merton's words, "communication" to "communion," from speaking with one another to being one with each other at the deepest level of encounter.[22]

Judging from the reactions to this whole event from all those present, it more than lived up to this expectation. I remember the Dalai Lama telling me about the first Gethsemani Encounter and the impact it had on him. He felt it was a very significant and substantive development. He found it personally gratifying to be involved with these monastics from both traditions, an activity he thoroughly enjoyed. Meeting with members of Christian monastic communities is one of the most treasured aspects of his life. It is something to which he looks forward.

GETHSEMANI ENCOUNTER II

Gethsemani Encounter II built on the historically important event of July 1996. Capturing the spirit of the gathering, *MID* published a report of it in its periodical, the *Bulletin*, and some months after this text was written, the proceedings appeared in print under the title *Transforming Suffering: Reflections on Finding Peace in Troubled Times*.[23]

The Second Gethsemani Encounter met again April 13–18, 2002, at the Abbey of Gethsemani, the Trappist monastery near Louisville in Nelson County, Kentucky. There were some sixty participants, with twenty Buddhists coming from the three traditions of Zen, Vajrayana (Tibetan), and Theravada. They were joined by twelve current and four former MID members and seven of its advisers, as well as some guests. A number of the monks from the Gethsemani community also took part in the dialogues.

The topic of discussion at Gethsemani II was suffering and its relationship to transformation, how both traditions regard these realities. The presentations and the conversations focused on four primary causes of suffering in our time: (1) a feeling of alienation and unworthiness, (2) the suffering caused by consumerism and greed, (3) the suffering stemming from structural and personal violence, and (4) the natural suffering associated with the process of aging, illness, and the inevitable approach of death.[24]

Abbot Thomas Keating, who gave the keynote for the Christian side, spoke about the suffering that arises from the operation of the false self, the illusions it generates, and the radical nature of love that transforms us. He described how comprehensive is the change when we are freed from the false self and its hidden programs for happiness. When this freedom is born or becomes operative, the transformation from the false self system is complete. When that happens, love penetrates all aspects of our life and being.[25]

The Venerable Henepola Gunaratana, the Buddhist keynote speaker, who is from the Bhavana Society, a Buddhist community in the Theravada tradition in West Virginia, in his talk reflected on the question of why suffering exists, concluding that it results from our over-identification with the self. Maintaining and defending the classical Buddhist view, he states that suffering happens "because of the core of clinging, or attachment to self.[26] He goes on to suggest the practice of loving-kindness, or *metta*, as an antidote and an effective way to mitigate personal suffering.[27]

Thomas Ryan, a Paulist priest who is the director of the Paulist Office for Ecumenical and Interfaith Relations in New York City and an adviser to MID, also attended Gethsemani II. He had this to say of the event:

> They began each conversation with the musical and meditative interlude of a recorder, but the openness and sensitivity of the conver-

sation itself became the real music. They didn't solve a single problem, but they kindled a vital force—friendship—with which to confront problems together in the future.[28]

In terms of Gethsemani II's attempt to understand suffering as a path to transformation, Tom Ryan concludes, "Both traditions of spiritual practice recognize . . . that *the way we live through* the experience of suffering is what makes it a path to transformation."[29] It is our response to suffering that determines whether it will be beneficial for us in the long run, and our response will depend in great measure on our spiritual development.

Finally, Abbot John Daido Loori offered a profound, perspective-generating insight that uncovers common ground in our shared humanity. He observed with luminous clarity and simplicity, "In the critical moments of life and death, we transcend traditions. Whatever we do, regardless of method, it is the heart behind it that matters."[30] In these nitty-gritty times in our lives, we are stripped of all differences, since they no longer matter, and face our essential equality before the Divine Mystery.

HINDU–CHRISTIAN DIALOGUE

The Hindu-Christian conversation has been going on irregularly since the mid-1700s, initiated by the Jesuit missionaries to the subcontinent, under the inspired leadership of the Italian Jesuit, Roberto de Nobili (1577–1656), who had learned Sanskrit and assumed sannyasa, or Indian monastic life as a renunciant.[31] There was a conservative reaction in some segments of the Indian church, and the encounter and dialogue declined until the latter decades of the nineteenth century. Brahma-bandhab Upadhyay (1861–1907), a brilliant, charismatic Brahmin convert to Catholicism, who was initiated as a Christian sannyasi, greatly stimulated the Christian-Hindu conversation on a mystical level and was a vitally important pioneering figure in the development of what came to be called *inculturation*, the movement to adapt the Christian faith to the culture, language, symbols, gestures, theology, and spirituality of a particular culture, in this early instance, in India.[32] He played a major role in developing an Indian Christian theology that was wholly Christian and wholly Indian. His vision has guided this process of evolution in Christian thought in India ever since.

The contacts between Christians and Hindus unfolded through regular forums such as small conferences, seminars, workshops, dialogues, and the very popular live-in retreats. The latter in particular, similar to the Gethsemani Encounters, were occasions of sharing from a very profound mystical depth, an openness on the part of the participants to the contemplative wisdom of each tradition. There was something more in these encounters that was not present in the Christian-Buddhist monastic experience to date, with rare exceptions: All the Christian figures who have been engaged in this encounter and existential dialogue have been greatly influenced in their spiritual lives by it. The genius of Indian spirituality and mysticism has passed into their Christian contemplative life. It is more than dialogue; it is convergence. A new culture is being born that is both Hindu and Christian or, more precisely, Indian and Christian.

Jules Monchanin (1895–1957),[33] a French priest who moved to South India from France in 1938 to explore the Hindu mystical tradition and who related the depths of Christian wisdom to this Hindu contemplative experience, founded Shantivanam Ashram, a Christian monastic community expressed through the culture of India, with Henri Le Saux (1910–1973),[34] a French Benedictine, who joined him in 1948. Both became Christian sannyasis, and Le Saux assumed the Indian name of Abhishiktananda, or Bliss of the Anointed One or, more loosely translated, Bliss of Christ. Together they established Shantivanam in 1950 as the first attempt at Western monastic life in an Indian/Hindu context. Their whole purpose was to relate inwardly, in the depths of inner experience, Hindu *advaita*, or nondual mysticism, with the living reality of the Trinity. This has been the ideal of Indian mystical theology ever since.

Monchanin died in 1957, and Abhishiktananda remained the head of Shantivanam until 1968, when he turned it over to Bede Griffiths and retired to a more contemplative life in his hermitage in Uttarkashi in the Himalayas. He died in 1973, but his influence on the Hindu-Christian relationship continues to be felt. He, more than any other Christian and monastic, as a mystic in the subcontinent, plunged into the inner reality of Upanishadic mysticism, the eternal inspiration of Indian seers. There, in those ultimate reaches of divinity, which he accessed experientially, he attempted to relate his Christian faith to those incomprehensible realities.[35] He was a genuinely interspiritual or cross-cultural mystic. He was convinced that Christianity, in its essential, living core, could meet the challenge of advaita, or nondual awareness. He remarks:

Only Christianity—that is, in its ultimate experience of Spirit—can answer the dilemma posed by advaita to all the religions and philosophies of the world. Or rather, it will accept what is essential in the advaitic experience and penetrate to its very heart; and yet it will still remain itself, or even find itself anew precisely in those depths of the Spirit to which advaita recalls it.[36]

Numerous other bilateral dialogues, some of them ongoing, are being conducted with other traditions. We have earlier examined the one with the Jewish people, with Buddhism in its monastic dimension, and with Hinduism. There is also a rich dialogue with Islam, and warm, deep encounters are taking place in North America, Europe, and India. The Middle East would be another important area. The Holy See has been exploring the Catholic-Islamic relationship for many years, and a strong friendship exists. Archbishop Michael Fitzgerald, an Islamicist, is the president of the Pontifical Council for Interreligious Dialogue. No doubt, his talents will be tapped in fostering this relationship. Similarly, a strong relationship exists between the American church and the Native American community; this relationship has been evolving for years. How the Catholic Church relates to all the great world religions might well determine the fate of the world.

Part IV

THE HISTORICAL HORIZON OF
THE DIALOGUE'S POSSIBLE FUTURE

9

READING THE SIGNS OF THE TIMES

A Possible New Course for the Catholic Church

During President Bill Clinton's first term, Daniel Golden, the administrator of the National Aeronautics and Space Administration (NASA) and a Clinton appointee, approached Father John Minogue, C.M., the president of Chicago's DePaul University, who was himself on NASA's board of directors, to assist him in organizing an advisory council for NASA composed of scholars representing all the religious traditions of humankind. I know this information from Jeffrey Carlson, who was at the time a dean of DePaul University and now is the dean at Dominican University in the Chicago area. He and I both serve on the board of the Parliament of the World's Religions and have become friends through interfaith work and our association through DePaul. Jeff was one of the scholars invited to join this advisory group, representing the Catholic tradition. He accepted the invitation, along with Father Minogue, and both were curious and enthusiastic about this assignment. Out of this relationship with DePaul University, where some of the NASA advisory council meetings have occurred, a special NASA center has been established at DePaul.

One of the questions Golden has put to the religious scholars is this: If tomorrow the government were to announce that we have made contact with extraterrestrials and are developing a relationship with them, what would be the reaction of your tradition and your constituents? I'm paraphrasing here, but you can imagine the impact of this question. The obvious reaction would be "Why are you interested in this question? What's behind it?"

This question raises a serious hypothetical situation for the Catholic Church. If such an event actually happened and extraterrestrials emerge into the mainstream of human experience, what impact would this have on the church's thinking? Let's be more daring in our imagined scenario of disclosure: We discover that not only have extraterrestrials been around for hundreds of millions of years, but they have a highly organized religion, a subtle theology, and a profound experience of God. What if it turned out that Christ, or the Divine Incarnate Logos, revealed himself to them two hundred million years ago and a church was established with a pontiff as its supreme teacher and leader? What effect would this revelation have on Vatican thinking, not to mention the whole of humanity?

Of course this scenario is quite bizarre, and most people wouldn't take it seriously. The question is, Are we willing to change in the face of new knowledge or new insight and wisdom? It may not be as extreme as this hypothetical extraterrestrial phenomenon, but it might be as challenging in its own way.

In this chapter, we will consider some of the signs of the times the church and its leadership must confront. Then a more ambitious role for the church vis-à-vis the other religions in promoting the Community of Religions will be considered, a possible new structure that will allow them to communicate, discuss on a regular or daily basis, and perhaps take collective initiatives. Then we will move on to outline a new model of the church in terms of its self-identity and its mission to the whole of the human family, or the church as matrix. In this context, we will examine the three options of the church and how it would operate as the matrix.

THE SIGNS OF THE TIMES

As in the early 1960s and the Second Vatican Council, and other instances in its preceding history, the Catholic Church has reached a moment in time when it must again read the signs of the times, since important decisions of direction have to be taken. Our age has witnessed numerous developments that it needs to acknowledge and appreciate if we are to progress as church, as human community in solidarity with all sentient beings who share this world with us, and as planet. These signs of the times include (1) the sexual abuse scandal, (2) the role of the laity in the church, (3) the women's issue, (4) the environment, (5) violence, terrorism, and war, (6) corruption in corporate capitalism, and a fundamental flaw in the system, (7) the disparity between the haves and the have-nots, (8) political oppression, and (9) the interfaith movement.

These are just the major ones with which the Catholic Church must be concerned and to which it must positively relate. Some of these issues are in-house, while the remaining concern all of humankind.

THE SEXUAL ABUSE MATTER

All of the concerns mentioned in this list are very important, but perhaps none goes to the heart of the Catholic Church's credibility and authority quite like the sexual abuse problem. The damage caused to the church's reputation by the actions of accused priests has been incalculable. There has been a drop-off of attendance at Mass, and some candidates for ordination have left, not wishing to commit themselves to a church with such corruption having been covered up. The justified anger aroused among the faithful, and beyond the domain of the church, has been intense, and the protests, shrill. Church leaders—from the pope, the curial officials, the College of Cardinals, to bishops and their priests—have felt the unbearable pressure of this rising anger and are demanding, not asking for, radical reform. The church leadership is keenly aware that weak measures will only be met with scorn and criticism, and they would further weaken the church's position in society and globally. The church is profoundly aware of the gravity pedophilia represents and so is taking steps to screen out such candidates for the priesthood and, where abuse occurs, to deal with it forcefully, comprehensively, and decisively, not tolerating even a suggestion of cover-up. The actions of Rome and the American bishops have shown this direction to be the case. The guidelines and measures they have adopted are a major step forward from this very dark period in the church's history.

A bit of historical clarification might be helpful here. In the late 1970s and early 1980s, the church was just beginning to become more informed about the psychological dynamics of the compulsion of pedophilia and sexual misconduct involving postpubescent teenagers. Until that time, church authorities had little understanding of the pathological nature of abusers. The church's theology of sin viewed sexual abuse as a grave sin or morally reprehensible. Because the church has always followed the imperative of protecting the flock from any hint of scandal, which could damage faith, accused priests were reassigned, particularly those priests who were actually guilty of these wicked deeds. This was the common practice until the hierarchy became better educated about the pathology involved and the moral/legal issues raised by actual instances of acting out.

The old culture of secrecy, meant to safeguard the faith of Catholics, ended up creating the milieu of cover-up that we have now painfully witnessed, with its resultant catastrophic aftermath to the psychological condition of victims and the financial/public relations nightmare for the Catholic Church in the United States. If the church wishes to regain its moral authority in the United States and around the world, it must honestly face this critical matter to the satisfaction of the people, church or canon law, and civil law. There is no doubt in my mind that the church is doing all in its power to correct this terrible situation. More and more there is the realization among church leaders, as among all the faithful, that there is no higher priority, in this context, than the safety of our children. Emphasis must be given to the victims, especially to the promotion of their complete healing.

THE ROLE OF THE LAITY IN THE CHURCH

There is a recognition all around the church that the people should have a larger role in deciding who the leaders of the church will be, or at least a say in the process of selecting them. In the instance of the sexual misconduct issue, the laity have played a significant role in keeping the pressure on the church leadership to move toward the requisite solutions. Their contribution was effective and positive, demonstrating that their wisdom, clarity, sincerity, and determination can be trusted.

I believe the time has come when the people have to be enfranchised—that is, given the right and the responsibility to elect the pope. There is no necessity to continue with the elitist policy of confining the election of the successor of Peter to the College of Cardinals. I do feel that the cardinals can have a function in the election, but it should be limited to confirming the people's choice. When it comes to the selection of bishops, again the people should be given some responsibility, perhaps to nominate candidates or at least to be able to vote on the ones Rome chooses.

On every level of ecclesial life, the laity should have a central voice. This view means that the faithful who are sufficiently qualified would be permitted to serve in the government of the Universal Church and in the regional or national conferences of bishops and the government of dioceses everywhere. The talents of qualified laity can be tapped in various forums of the church's ministry and outreach. Reform in the area of the laity's role will not happen easily and will no doubt involve considerable struggle and debate.

THE WOMEN'S ISSUE

In many ways, the issue of the place of women in the Catholic Church is potentially as serious—or should be—as the sexual misconduct cover-up. Most women in the church are not willing to be silent any longer. So many women are immensely gifted with intellect, vision, educational skills, and natural leadership qualities. We have seen these qualities among women in India, Pakistan, Bangladesh, Sri Lanka, and Great Britain, where women have all been elected prime minister of their respective nations. Considerable momentum exists, especially in the United States and Canada, to honestly debate the role of women in the church and not to foreclose this issue. Most urgently, there is the question of women being called to ordination. Pope John Paul II has closed the door to this possibility, but few feel that his declarations on this issue settle the matter for all time. One objection is that the theological reasoning of the pope and other ecclesial leaders has been very unconvincing. The issue of women and their place in the church will not go away until real justice exists in the church.

THE CONTINUING ECOLOGICAL CRISIS

The progressive deterioration of the environment that we are witnessing, the grave problem of the decline of biodiversity as more and more precious species become extinct because of the irresponsible actions of the human species, the disappearance of clean water, rich soil, and unpolluted air, are all deeply disturbing trends that are harbingers of a difficult future for life on Earth. The magnitude of this problem exceeds human calculation. It is beyond doubt the primary moral crisis of our age, since the fate of the Earth will settle all other merely human concerns. We need to focus on this crisis, and the church, I believe, has to take a leadership role in educating the faithful and the world population in what precisely is expected of each one of us, for we have all contributed to this nightmare fast approaching on all sides. More and more I am of the view that the Catholic Church's ascetical teaching should be emphasized, applying it to the realm of consumption and encouraging everyone to embrace voluntarily simplicity of life, with less and less unnecessary consumption. We must simplify our lives. We no longer have a choice in this matter, if we want to survive on this precious island in the cosmos. I believe it is still not too late for humankind.

VIOLENCE, TERRORISM, AND WAR

Terrible acts of violence in our societies and terrorist campaigns, mostly in Israel and the West, are commonplace. The Iraqi war has occasioned a vast outpouring of humanity against war. This international effort was impressive and historic because it represented a new moment in history where people were asserting themselves from every corner of the earth. For the first time in historical memory, most of humanity was making its voice heard virtually everywhere.

The roots of war and terrorism are found in old antagonisms and new situations of mistrust, as in the Middle East. The deeper causes of war and terrorism are fear and ignorance, and in terms of the systematic violence of war, it is often the greed or ambition of a ruling few who drag the people into wars they don't want or countenance. Much of the frenzy that violence represents is taught and reinforced by the entertainment media, which gives us a steady diet of violent images and scenarios in movie after movie, TV series, miniseries, and violent games for our children. This matter should cause us real concern and stimulate the desire to take direct action of a moral and legal kind.

Here again, the church needs to assert its voice and example. It needs to challenge the media to be more responsible. There is a wonderful and long witness of the church to peace and even, with Pope John Paul II, an espousal of nonviolence. The church can become the focus of the world's desire for peace and a world devoid of terrorism and guns.

A CORRUPT CORPORATE CAPITALISM

Capitalism is becoming a serious issue in the United States with the Enron and Worldcom scandals. These corporations have revealed an ugly side to corporate capitalism, how self-serving it can be for the select few at the top to the detriment of the employees and, in these and other instances, the unwary stockholders. We see in these instances the need for reform of this institution, and such reform is an immense task that requires a redefinition of capitalism itself.

The corrupt practices of capitalism are only one dimension of the problem. There is a flaw, from the perspective of the Gospel and simple fairness, in the very conception of capitalism itself, especially in its concrete practice.

This is not an issue the church needs to be tutored in to be sufficiently conscious of, since the hierarchy, particularly John Paul II, has been a sharp critic of the ways an unruly capitalism operates. Again and again, in encyclicals and other public discourses, the pope has taught the basic injustice of the capitalistic system as it impacts so negatively on three-fourths of humanity that lives in utter poverty, and most in destitution. In the papal concern expressed on so many occasions, the pontiff was also following the clear directions of the church's very well developed social justice teaching. The pope's teaching has been as eloquent as it has been persistent. This is a sign of the times that the church has grasped long before the rest of the world. In this realization, the church has aligned itself with the poor and with the future of humanity where society works for everyone. The church has always known in the modern experience that a society, a civilization, cannot work for all persons if it rests on a system that encourages greed and often results in corruption. The church will continue to emphasize these sober kinds of truth on the level of practical life.

DISPARITY BETWEEN THE HAVES AND HAVE-NOTS

Closely related to the issue of capitalism and the necessity for its reform, since capitalism has helped produce the huge division between the wealthy and the poor, is the horrendous problem of the gap between those who have resources and those who do not. The gulf between the rich and poor grows steadily greater with each passing year. Ultimately, there can be no lasting peace if there is no real social justice.

Social justice minimally requires an economic system that includes everybody. Again, this is an issue the church has been very sensitive to for decades, at least since the pontificate of Leo XIII (1878). A system that looks the other way and doesn't address the disparity that exists is one that is inherently antithetical to the Gospel and so is at war with the vision of the Kingdom of God that the church proclaims. Recent popes have attempted to apply in the aspiration of a Civilization of Love as both Paul VI and John Paul II have taught. The church will undoubtedly continue to be a voice for the have-nots, who are essentially completely voiceless in themselves. In all of this, the church has embraced an option for the poor.

POLITICAL OPPRESSION

The continuing tragedy of political and economic oppression is a concern the church gives voice to more vigorously than it has in the past; however, more can be done. The church is very good at expressing support for the victims of oppressive regimes in the abstract when it doesn't cost very much, but it has not always been helpful in the concrete. For example, the church has not uttered a word in support of the overwhelming suffering of the Tibetan people. It has absented itself from this moral struggle, leaving it to others to represent this noble people. The Dalai Lama has met with many Catholic leaders over the last few decades, including Paul VI and John Paul II. He has had at least four or five substantive talks with John Paul, and although the pope is sympathetic to the Tibetan people, he has not made any public statements about the oppressive conditions the Tibetan people have been living under since 1949. While it is surely the case that the church is deeply committed to the freedom of all nations and cultures, and the fundamental rights of all people, and it has expressed these sentiments in many documents, it hasn't done enough to challenge dictators and other oppressors. This remains an area the church needs to consider. It must be a vehicle for advocating the political, social, economic, and educational enfranchisement of all oppressed peoples.[1]

THE INTERFAITH MOVEMENT

As we have seen throughout this book, the Catholic Church takes relations with the other religions very seriously, and it is a primary leader in the meeting of the various religions. The interfaith movement is a revolution in slow motion spreading among the nations and cultures of the world. It has an implication for the church, an implication that a new age has dawned in which the religions must work together and find ways to add collectively their moral authority to the future shape of global civilization. The interfaith movement is growing in leaps and bounds, and it requires institutions and an international structure that will facilitate the smooth communication among the religious and spiritual leaders of the planet, allowing for their orchestration of collective collaborative action and the support of projects in service to humanity.

The encounter of the religions or the interfaith phenomenon will not disappear; it is here to stay and is part of the planet's future and its universal culture. The church has played a very crucial role in the birth and growth of the interfaith emergence into world history. It cannot control this development or hinder its progress. It's an idea whose time has come. Obstructing this movement or trying to reverse it won't work, nor will lukewarm support serve the church's ultimate purpose. Church leaders have to face the facts. It can be said that the interfaith reality is the work of the Holy Spirit, and the church has an opportunity here to take leadership in a radical way.

THE CHURCH AS ARCHITECT
OF THE COMMUNITY OF RELIGIONS

The interfaith movement has reached a point where a more substantial and flexible institutional structure is required to assist the work of inter-religious dialogue, collaboration, and prophetic action taken together for the sake of justice; peace; the environment; clarification of bioethical is-sues; the reform of capitalism and globalization; the closing of the gap between the rich and the poor nations; the promotion of the rights of all, especially women and children; the spread of education and univer-sal health care, with accessible medicines; the enhancement of employ-ment opportunities; and the abandonment of child labor. An interna-tional organization is necessary to provide a structure in which the world's religions, with other guiding institutions, representing science, government, civil society, commerce, the media, and nongovernmental organizations (NGOs), can meet on a regular basis and discuss all the critical issues, while developing the habit of working together, building up a culture of peace and community among the members.

Such an enterprise is greatly needed today, since the interfaith or-ganizations, such as the World Conference on Religion and Peace, the Parliament of the World's Religions, the Temple of Understanding, the World Congress of Faiths, the Fellowship of Reconciliation, and the United Religions Initiative, are not sufficient to meet the task and the vast needs of the religions and related organizations to interact on a daily basis. There is a further essential point here to consider: None of these interfaith organizations were actually founded by the religions or in any way reflect an initiative by them, together or unilaterally. Nor can the existing interfaith organizations speak for the religions; they don't have the authority. All they can do is provide a forum for religious and spiri-tual leaders and others to meet, giving input and providing experts. They often refuse to take a stand or take risks. For these reasons, I believe the Catholic Church has an important historic opportunity to initiate a process resulting in the world's religions together founding an interna-tional organization to represent them and reflect their hopes for the fu-ture of our planet in its great diversity and cultural/spiritual richness.

This new organization would be in effect the Community of Re-ligions, which would also, more precisely, be a Community of Commu-nities, since the religions are themselves communities of faith within the body of the larger human community. It is given this name of Commu-nity of Religions to advance the model and ideal of community itself, the new model of how the religions are relating to one another, and the ideal of developing more and more bonds of connection and friendship between and among themselves. The new model replaces the old one of mutual suspicion, competition, and conflict, the basis of thousands of wars throughout history. The church, as a major community of faith and as initiator of the Community of Religions, the international structure dedicated to interreligious communication in all areas of life, becomes through its call to the other religions a central, inspiring voice and presence within the official organism of the world's great religions. Calling into being the global consciousness of the Community of Religions would be one of its primary goals.

Dialogue and collaboration are at the heart of the mission of this prospective interfaith organization. This organization would be dedicated to the supreme value and practice of dialogue, of interreligious conversation opening out into all sorts of collaboration. Dialogue characterizes the enduring teaching of the religions drawn together in this holy association. It has become their new and permanent way of being, acting, orientation, and attitude. Making peace among themselves and consecrating their dialogical mission through their example, the religions discover various ways to act together in collaborative projects. It is this double commitment to these principles—dialogue and collaboration—that the Community of Religions can contribute to the nations of the world. The nations of the world must learn to rely more and more on dialogue to resolve potential conflicts, and through such a resolution, to make possible genuine mutual kinds of collaboration.

Collaborative efforts would naturally foster global peace based on real justice, in a situation where the human family is also living in an enlightened harmony with the Earth, a harmonious relationship that is enhancing of the planet's systems, its air, water, soil, biodiversity, beauty, innate wisdom, and wilderness areas.[2] Out of its various dialogical activities in the Community of Religions, new relationships between members of this community would emerge. Individuals, groups, associations, small communities, centers, and other educational institutions would all work together in forging a new sense of humankind's greater identity beyond the religions standing alone as erstwhile cultures of isolation and often as forces fermenting misunderstanding, suspicion, hostility, and conflict.

Into this vastly new global situation of universal openness, where the bonds of amity and deep connections of community are being progressively discovered, the Catholic Church's mission becomes expressed and pursued with much greater subtlety than in the past two thousand years. Its language assumes an even greater importance as it strives to be more sensitive to the reality of diversity in an age of pluralism in which the church cannot dominate the other traditions with claims to a superior position of Truth and the means of salvation, even if these claims are ultimately true in the light of its mandate from Christ and the ontological depths and heights of reality's eternal purpose manifested through the Incarnation. The church has an overriding responsibility to be an agent of peace among all peoples, and it cannot contribute to tensions and divisions by insisting on its more ultimate position. The church, in the Interspiritual Age, is prompted by the Spirit to so shape its mission within the Community of Religions, that its unambiguous witness to the truth as it knows it is communicated through its presence and example.

This presence and example become, in the light of its self-understanding and the workings of grace in this new age, with its unique set of problems and opportunities, incarnated in the inspiring and effective outpouring of love that is characteristic of holiness of life. Its evangelizing mission becomes manifested primarily through its example, and those of its sons and daughters in the world, in the various situations of encounter that occur on all levels, especially in the dialogue of life itself, the ordinary exchanges between persons of different faiths in streets, neighborhoods, schools, in commercial settings, through friendships and civic associations, and pursuits through various organizations whose purpose is manifold. Such a new way of being and acting for the church is actually an external manifestation and concretization of its inner nature and truth, its ontological reality and spiritual destiny. It means the church must be now, and for all the ages to come, what Christ has meant it to be. Such a course of presence and example requires of its leadership great holiness of life, imagination, and immense sensitivity, a sensitivity that is at once a vast awareness and the highest expression of intelligence.

A question can legitimately be raised at this point: Does a document like *Dominus Iesus* help or hinder the pursuit of harmonious relations among the religions of the world, and thus contribute to universal peace, or does it complicate the situation by introducing tension into the church's relations with the various traditions in such a way that trust is diminished, and what has been gained from previous efforts has been cast into doubt? This is a question for church leaders to ponder. One point is quite clear in this age: We must be very, very careful what we proclaim to the world. There has to be a balance between the imperative of the

evangelical mandate of the church given by Christ and the universal demands of peace. Everything today depends on furthering the prospects
for such a pervasive and lasting peace. Without it, everything may be
lost. In the light of this stark, sobering realization, the church's behavior
in other ages becomes problematic in the Interspiritual Age, which has
its own paradoxes and necessities. It seems immoral to be pushing theological superiority if it contributes ultimately to the breakdown of peace
and the horrendous prospect of a clash of civilizations. We must never
forget—no matter who we are—that words have often started wars, and
the church is an institution that depends on the use of words, as all institutions do. All the more reason for the leadership of the church, the
Magisterium, to choose their words with great care, concern, humility,
discretion, a spacious generosity, compassion, love, and profound, even
supernatural, kindness.

The nature, structure, purpose, and goals of the Community of Religions can only be determined by the participating religions of the
world, but here are some indications. The inner motivating being of this
organization is essentially the realization of the unity of the human family, the ontological interdependence of all its cultures, religions, nations,
and members. There is economic, social, political, scientific, philosophical, cultural, and spiritual interdependence because there is a unity of being from which springs the interconnection of all of us. This realization,
and the necessity for the survival of our precious planet, serves to moti-
vate the religions to form the Community of Religions.

The structure of this prospective organization will have to reflect the
richness of its membership. It cannot be conceived in simply Western
terms; it must strive for an organizational shape that gives life and expression to the spiritual genius that inspires each tradition. All the traditions, admitted into membership in the Community of Religions, would
enjoy an essential equality and the rights associated with it. These of
course will be elaborated in its charter and other founding documents.
No particular tradition can have a dominant role over the others, but each
is a full participant in the community, with an equal vote. All must share
the rights and the responsibilities of membership, however these are formulated and whatever their final form. Most likely, leadership would be
on a rotating basis, with all the members represented on the governing
council. Various levels of institutional structure will be required to carry
out the multidimensional tasks of the Community of Religions.

The basic purpose is to bring humankind together through the
guiding principles of dialogue and collaboration. It is to contribute to

the whole world moral, spiritual, and visionary leadership to inspire in the human family a positive direction away from the destructive course of the past. It is to appeal to the best in humanity, to draw the planet ever more toward the ideal of universal culture, which would be the Culture of cultures. In this effort the community would have recourse to build upon all the foundational documents of the United Nations (i.e., the UN Charter, the Universal Declaration on the Rights of Man, UNESCO's "Declaration on the Role of Religion in the Promotion of a Culture of Peace"[3]), the Parliament's "Towards a Global Ethic: An Initial Declaration"[4] and "A Call to Our Guiding Institutions,"[5] and Monastic Interreligious Dialogue's the Universal Declaration on Nonviolence,[6] to mention a few.

The goals of the Community of Religions are manifold and of course will change in the unfolding of future history and the needs of each succeeding age, though some of the these may be perennial concerns. These include the assiduous pursuit of peace, the struggle for justice, the promotion of the rights of all people and the rights of other sentient beings, the disciplined work for ecological responsibility and justice, and the long-term commitment to building a civilization of love, a new universal society with a heart. This goal, as we have seen, was born as a vision of hope of Pope Paul VI and was pursued by him during his pontificate and that of Pope John Paul II.

Membership, in addition to all the religions of the world, will also be extended to the interfaith organizations: the Parliament of the World's Religions, also called the Council for a Parliament of the World's Religions (CPWR), the Temple of Understanding, the World Congress of Faiths, the World Conference on Religion and Peace, and the United Religions Initiative. Membership will also be open to the other guiding institutions of our societies: governments, labor and commerce, or the corporate segment, higher education, arts and media, science and health care, NGOs, and others. How these organizations and influential institutions will interact within the community, and what functions they will serve, will be decided by the members of the community themselves.

THE CHURCH AS MATRIX: A NEW MODEL

Although it is not always apparent, there is in Catholicism a dynamism at its core; there is a vitality and a hidden strength, a vital capacity to assimilate and learn from other faiths and cultures, to understand the scientific, philosophical, theological, and technological developments that emerge. Novelty is often initially disorienting, but once the church understands the nature of the advances, it is able to relate itself to the new situation. I believe the church is at a historic crossroads and faces three possible options.

The first option is not a very satisfactory one. It involves the church leadership looking to the past, seeking security in a former age of theological coherence, ecclesial dominance, and a Christian culture living in isolation from all others. These were ages in which the church controlled education, and life was at a much slower pace and simpler. If the church is taken back to the past, it will lose credibility and influence in the present and the future, and its effectiveness will be diminished.

The second option is just as undesirable, since it would have the church react to the present in light of the past. New developments might be rejected, developments of a cultural, theological, dialogical, and scientific nature. Reacting to present and future developments through the lens of past certitudes, and rigidly resisting necessary change and advances in our understanding could hamper the church, with similar results: a serious erosion of support for the church and continued loss of its credibility, authority, and influence.

The first and second options are understandable but unwise. Escape or reaction are temptations for the church, but they are not real options; they would only create more problems for the Catholic community.

The third option would see the church leadership reading the signs of the times, as Pope John XXIII did in his time when he proceeded to call the Second Vatican Council. Doing so would illuminate the church's situation vis-à-vis its own flock, the other traditions, the contemporary world, and what is required of its followers if it is to be of service to the future of humanity. Reading the signs of the times, the church would realize that the interfaith movement is now a permanent reality that will inevitably influence the future course of the world; the ecological crisis demands leadership from the church; the oppression of the Tibetan people requires a courageous voice in Rome; the moral vacuity of capitalism and all the harm it has done around the planet, and even to the planet, calls the church to a continuity of its critique of the capitalist system, globalization, and its witness to the poor. It will also notice the hope of women and their rising expectations, which can no longer be frustrated. These developments and others will invite the church and its leaders to adjust the Christian community to these realities. Its adjustments will emphasize continuity in the midst of change.

The third option entails a new model of the Catholic Church: the church as the matrix. A matrix is a container in which developments occur; it protects these changes, nurtures them, and allows them to grow unhindered by negative influences from outside. The term *matrix* derives from the Latin root of *mater*, meaning "mother." A mother also protects and nurtures the unborn in her womb and guards against harmful factors from the surrounding environment.

Reading the signs of the times, and realizing the potential of the church to contribute in all these areas and many others besides, the church can relate itself positively to all these concerns in such a way that it nourishes the hopes of humanity and is an advocate in resolving all the critical issues the human family faces in common: the ecological crisis, war and peace, violence and terrorism, global homelessness, the plight of refugees, the reform of capitalism, development in the poorer nations, economic equality and opportunity, and the harmony of the religions.

In its role and identity as matrix, the Catholic Church becomes a welcoming, reconciling, and healing presence in our divided world. Every person on this planet should feel a sense of real connection with the church because it is a beacon drawing humanity home. Just as the Jewish people now have a special relationship with the church—and this relationship can be seen as a model for all other religious communities— the church in this new age can make room for everyone. This approach is a definite and real expectation of the matrix, a hope that is realizable. Taking this course, the church then becomes for the human family a vehicle to bring our world together.

If it can see its way to this quality of generosity, the church could be a great teacher of interspirituality, being in itself a spaciousness that takes in all that is genuine in humanity's experience of the Ultimate Reality, the Divine, or Transcendent Mystery. Protecting the living spirituality, mysticism, and contemplative practices and insights of the various traditions, the church as matrix is enthusiastically open and responsive to the values and mystical/spiritual treasures of the world embedded in the cultures of humankind. This is the interspiritual vision.

Interspirituality assumes a unity in humanity's experience of the Sacred. Although there are many differences of belief and practice among the faiths, the religions share this profound dimension of mystical consciousness. In an informal way, the existence of this dimension of experience in the human family, and the universal elements it contains, represent a universal wisdom, the *philosophia perennis*, and is the basis of a global spirituality, though this spirituality is neither intentional nor systematic. The fruits of the spiritual life, which emanate from all the streams of religious experience, are the same and can be summed up in holiness of life, and this holiness of being is expressed in compassion, kindness, mercy, love, and a spacious sensitivity. It can be observed that if the fruits are the same, then the Source who inspired them is also the same.

The Catholic Church also has these qualities of the spiritual life, and as the matrix, it can be described as exercising a spacious sensitivity in its attitude of openness and acceptance of otherness. This tender spaciousness of being, attitude, theology, and horizon prepares it to envision a Civilization of Love, or a universal society with a heart, a global polity conceived and founded on compassion and caring, sharing, and commitment to one another, where it all works for everyone, not just a minority of humanity. The church would promote this vision in all of its activities, as it has been doing more selectively for some time now. Anything short of this kind of vision would reduce the influence, role, and effectiveness of the church in its mission to the whole world in our time.

10

THE CATHOLIC CHURCH AND
THE CRISIS OF THE WORLD

Every direction in which we look in our time there is crisis. We see it in the Catholic Church with the sexual abuse scandal and the damage it has caused to its authority and credibility. It is clear the planet is in extremity ecologically, and this situation was caused by the human species. There is a festering crisis in humanity itself, a crisis that is multifaceted: civilizational or cultural, political, economic, social, and spiritual. Each of these crises can have a genuine solution, but the work and sacrifice required are enormous; the imagination and vision, subtle; and the stamina, long-term. In the process of discovering solutions and in the effort to educate the human family, the Catholic Church can play a clear and decisive role.

For some time now I have been reflecting on the future of the church and the huge problems the world faces. It has occurred to me in this period in which the church is being criticized that given the levels of crisis the world is in, the extraordinary complexity and depth of it, the world will not survive without the church. It can also be observed that the fate of the Catholic Church is connected with the fate of the Earth itself. There is so much the church has learned in its more than two thousand years of history that would be useful to humanity in its attempt to navigate through this very dangerous and uncertain period in which we find ourselves.

The church's qualities are numerous, attributes of its earthly sojourn that can be drawn on in its contribution to building a new life for the planet in which all benefit. These attributes include (1) organizational skills; (2) diplomatic gifts; (3) abilities and insights into community, which the world needs; (4) vast mystical experience housed in the lives of its saints, contemplatives, and mystics and in more than fifty thousand books devoted to spirituality; (5) its deep commitment to peace, social justice, a capitalism and socialism that serve humanity, and ecological awareness; (6) its equally vast intellectual accomplishments in virtually every aspect of culture, especially in philosophy, theology, science, and literature; (7) its millions of saints who have greatly impacted the world; (8) its capacity for vision—for instance, in its notion of a Civilization of Love, a universal society with a heart; (9) its commitment to the unity of the human family, with its destiny for eternal beatitude; (10) its profound attachment to prayer, spirituality, and transformation; (11) its divine humanism evident in those who achieve a degree of maturity in the Christian life; and (12) its ultimate optimism for the world and humankind reflected in its pursuit of dialogue and cooperation with the other religions. If all of these qualities are seen as operative in the Catholic Church as the matrix, the divine community embracing everyone and creating a world order that works for everyone, then I believe the church may well provide the answer for our planet.

In this final chapter, we will look at the crisis of the world and characterize it briefly, especially the extremity in the ecological dimension of the Earth, which is the most serious one we face, and the crisis of humanity itself. These are the primary critical issues of the third millennium. Then there are the many divisions oppressing humankind: the gap between the poor, or have-nots, and the wealthy, or the haves; the dangers of religious division, carrying with it the possibility of a clash of civilizations, and the ruptures that can occur as a result of a kind of neoimperialism, such as we have seen with the exercise of American power. Then we will move on to consider the Catholic Church's possible contribution in relation to Islam. Some exploration of the church as a sacrament of reconciliation will be examined, which will integrate its outreach to Islam and the other faiths, with the chief means to achieve it, the gift of dialogue itself.

CHARACTERIZATION OF THE CRISIS OF THE WORLD

The planet is quickly reaching a turning point, where crucial decisions must be made. This is a dangerously unstable period in our history, and multidimensional challenges face us. The most pressing of the critical issues, and the one that takes priority over all the others, is the environmental crisis. Everything depends on resolving it in a satisfactory way. So many steps can be taken, some of which have been and others that are in process: conserving energy and discovering alternative sources of energy that are sustainable; repairing the quality of air through clearing up the pollution by higher standards of control; purifying the water supply by regulating dumping and the use of chemicals by industry. Most essentially, fundamental changes are required in how we live—that is, greatly simplifying our consumption and style of life. At this point, it does not seem humanity has the will to embrace simplicity of lifestyle. This whole area is the priority for the foreseeable future.

Then there are the multiple crises in humankind itself, and these are economic and cultural, with attendant political consequences and requirements. The major economic and social crisis is centered around the great disparity between the haves and the have-nots, or between the three-quarters of the human family living in poverty and destitution, and the quarter living in relative wealth, and the well-being it makes possible in the temporalities of life. Part of the destitute population is the more than one billion homeless persons living around the world. This situation is an immense critical problem in itself.

The cultural crisis, which has become all the more urgent since the events of September 11, 2001, and the violent reaction by the United States and a coalition of nations in Afghanistan, and later in Iraq, is really a problem of perception and worldview: the potential clash of civilizations. The difference of perspective is governed by profound considerations of culture and religion, of modernity versus a medieval view. The division here is between an extreme view of Islam by politically radical Muslims and the Western world led by the United States. Part of the problem is an unwillingness to allow cultural evolution in Islamic nations in line with the advances in modern life, including greater tolerance for diversity, and the freedom of ideas, expression, and independent thought/action that come with democracy. Extreme political Islam, a small minority of the Islamic community, is reacting against modern culture and some of the policies of the United States, such as its support for Israel with hardly any concern for the Palestinians. The insensitivity of U.S. policy and action has resulted in an intense hostility toward the United States by these militant factions, mostly from Arab countries.

The further threat of a clash of civilizations also takes the form of conflict between Christianity and Islam, since there is an intolerance toward Christians in some Arab societies, notably in Algeria and in Sudan, in which deeply disturbing trends have been developing in recent years. In Algeria, for instance, the very conservative Islam existing in that region, and the intolerance of some, led to the death of some French

Trappist monks who had a contemplative monastery there. Some Muslim countries express an unwillingness to accord Christians the same rights Muslims enjoy in Christian countries, as in Europe and North America. There is no reciprocity of religious rights.

Southern Sudan faces the frightful situation of an Islamic northern government persecuting a southern Christian population. This policy of persecution, however, has become a full-scale genocide against Christians. This is horrific and intolerable, yet little outcry from the rest of the world is heard. Although social, economic, and political factors are undoubtedly involved in this situation, there is a confrontation between two religious communities here, which is very troubling in its implications and in the suffering of those involved.

A further crisis the world faces is the emergence of a kind of neoimperialism primarily associated with the United States, especially since September 11, 2001, and its aftermath with the rise of an atmosphere of fear, heightened security to the detriment of personal freedoms, a palpable anxiety that has become part of life in the United States and the West more generally. As other nations regard U.S. actions, they are becoming apprehensive, since the United States' moral high ground seems to have been traded for a more menacing, bullying role for the only remaining superpower. Some see this new approach to U.S. power to be guided by a determination to reshape the world to its liking, regardless of the consequences to the conventions of the international community and the agreements by which civilized humanity lives. Many nations are worried by the ambition in Washington of imposing the Pax Americana.

THE POSSIBLE CONTRIBUTION
OF THE CATHOLIC CHURCH

The overriding challenge of this new age we have entered is this: how to become a unified world established in a global or universal civilization with a heart, a Civilization of Love, the very dream of the church itself expressed by its recent popes. This is the overarching goal and priority of the Catholic Church in this period of history since Vatican II, and it is a priority beyond its mandate to proclaim the Gospel, yet it is related. A Civilization of Love would be a universal order whose ideal is inspired by the Gospel itself, extending its vision to fructify in the lives of the masses of humanity.

If this vision became a reality around the globe and gripped the consciousness of the international community, then most of the problems we now face would find positive resolution, because most of the world's critical issues are the consequence of a lack of love or human ignorance, as is the case with much of the ecological crisis. Even this crisis could be solved if people were motivated from an unselfish desire to love and share. If we were committed to unselfish love in thought, word, and action, then we wouldn't pursue a life of consumption at the expense of the rest of humankind and the environment. We would learn to live with far less and just take what we actually need.

IMPACTING THE ENVIRONMENTAL CRISIS

In terms of the ecological dimension of the turning point the human family faces, the choice is fairly clear: Either change by way of simplifying our lives, or perish in an increasingly uncertain and hostile future. As I mentioned earlier, I don't think the human race has the will, at this point, to summon the wisdom and the stamina to change in time. We are such creatures of our bad habits, and the United States is the worst example here, especially with respect to extravagance and overindulgence. Simplicity of lifestyle doesn't seem to be part of the American character. We are so accustomed to abundance, but this abundance is for a comparatively few at the expense of the vast majority and the health of the planet itself. Here the Catholic Church can play a crucial role of fostering this change by educating its flock and the rest of humanity in the utter necessity of voluntary simplicity in how we live and use the goods of the Earth. The church has the educational skills and the resources to promote this kind of change.

THE CATHOLIC CHURCH'S CHALLENGE TO CAPITALISM

Related to this need for awakening to our ecological responsibility by adopting a more modest way of life in relation to the planet and to others is the very unjust economic situation of disparity, the huge separation between those who have the goods of this life and those who do not. The widening gap is partially the result of the intrinsic unfairness of the capitalist system, which, not being founded on or motivated by selfless love, justice, sharing, compassion, and an ethic of kindness, is ruthlessly habituated to manipulation of the conditions that maximize profits for a few and minimize benefits for the many. In this matter, the church has been and is a persistent and eloquent critic of an essentially irresponsible capitalism that is heartless, uncaring, economically cruel, and quite harsh. It is a system that ignores the long-term welfare of the Earth for the short-term fix it can acquire for itself. Its focus is not on the social impact of its economic pursuits but on filling the coffers of its stockholders and the corporate elite. The church leadership is well aware of all of this situation and what drives this morally reprehensible economic institution in its present state. The church seeks the reform of capitalism in such a way that integrity, a sense of responsibility to the Earth and the human family, would come to characterize its reformed nature as we enter more deeply into the third millennium. This new vision of the corporate world would also affect the nature and direction of globalization, the very extension of capitalism around the world.[1]

GUIDING THE AMERICAN SUPERPOWER

The church can also play a role in tempering the perhaps unruly and misguided American superpower, and it can do this by making available to the U.S. leadership the benefit of centuries of diplomatic experience, of insights culled from all manner of situations of interaction with kingdoms, empires, and, more recently, nation-states. It can share some of the wisdom it has acquired in the use of power and gently persuade the American authorities that there is a long-term view of history that requires wisdom and patience to understand it and to navigate through it. Just before the Iraq war in early spring 2003, Pope John Paul II tried unsuccessfully to guide President George W. Bush along another course, to dissuade him from invading Iraq, but to no avail. If, however, the church leadership would open up an ongoing dialogue with Washington, it may be able to convince the U.S. leadership that the same goals could be achieved in other ways.

PREVENTING A CLASH OF CIVILIZATIONS

John Paul II is profoundly committed to peace and nonviolence. He has consistently emphasized these values throughout his pontificate. That is why he vigorously opposed the United States over the war with Iraq and the Gulf War of 1991. This pontiff and the church were remaining true to their convictions, their central values of peacemaking and building a Civilization of Love. Another reason for the pope's leadership in the time leading up to the war was Rome's fear that such a war might precipitate a clash of civilizations. The papal action in opposing the war, along with the masses of Europe and the rest of the world, demonstrated to the Muslim nations that this war was not a clash of civilizations, not a war between the Christian and Muslim religions. John Paul's deft diplomacy and teaching undoubtedly helped prevent the war from getting out of control and becoming a confrontation between these two venerable traditions.

The Catholic Church has been and continues to be in a dialogue with Islam. It would be no exaggeration to say this dialogue began with St. Francis of Assisi and his celebrated encounter with the sultan of Egypt in the last years of the saint's life. Francis went to Egypt hoping to achieve martyrdom, and if not that prize, then to convert the sultan to the Christian faith. He succeeded in neither, but his apparent failure was also a victory of sorts because it exposed Muslims to a very advanced soul in holiness that has made a lasting impression in their historical memory. Francis discovered in the Islamic ruler someone devout in his faith, a sensitive person who was well educated and who could discern who Francis of Assisi was. A friendship was born in this significant encounter.

Nicholas of Cusa, or Cusanus, reinforced the desire for dialogue with Islam with the publication of his important work, *De Pace Fidei*,[2] which was completed in September 1453, just four months after the fall of Constantinople. Cardinal Cusanus advocated reconciliation, which of course required dialogue and a direct relationship. This work and the vision of Nicholas of Cusa represents a kind of turning point in the church's attitude toward Islam, though Cusanus was certainly way ahead of his time. There is in his example and inspiration an emphatic sense of direction, but it had to await another age to see its flowering—namely, the present age and on into the indefinite future. There is no doubt of the visionary status of Cusanus's radical approach, which saw the relationship of Christianity and Islam as resting on a unity of religion itself in the truth of God. There was a basis for peace (between the Christian world and Islam) in an existing harmony among the religions,[3] and pursuing the common roots could advance a lasting amity between the two faiths.

A good relationship exists between the Holy See and every Muslim nation. The Pontifical Council for Interreligious Dialogue has a special commission devoted to the Catholic Church's evolving relationship with Islam and with Muslims, the Commission for Religious Relations with Muslims. Its focus is to promote and conduct studies of all aspects and dimensions of the relationship between the two traditions. The president of the PCID and the commission is Archbishop Michael Fitzgerald, and he is well prepared for the dialogue with Islam, since he is himself an Islamicist. He also has considerable experience in interreligious dialogue, especially with Muslim scholars, figures, and religious leaders. Archbishop Fitzgerald has been a member of the PCID, including overseeing it for many years. Deep, subtle, warm dialogical relations exist between the Vatican through the PCID and Islamic groups, primarily in the Middle East. This position is very important for the future stability of the world and offers an opportunity for the church to play a substantial role in this vital area.

Over the past two millennia, the Catholic Church has acquired considerable experience in organizing and teaching, and it has learned how to guard the teaching center of the faith from destructive voices that might try to distort or change the deposit of faith, especially the doctrines mentioned in the Creed. Church authorities have evolved a system in which the leadership speaks with one voice, and normally there are never any contradictions in the exercise of this unified voice; that is, different figures are not making statements at odds with one another. This is a very important skill for a government, and crucial for a religion, if confusion is to be avoided.

The Catholic's Church voice has traditionally been and continues to be the Magisterium, especially as this teaching authority emanates from the pope himself. The pope exercises a supreme teaching authority in the Catholic understanding of Christianity. This central authority gives cohesion to the faith and the countless institutions of the church spread throughout the world. An important, even critical, lesson for other faiths is evident here, particularly for Islam, which suffers from too many voices claiming to rightly interpret the Qur'an and so guide the *ummah*, the Islamic commonwealth.

Islam needs not so much a supreme leader as an ultimate authority vested in an international assembly that represents all segments of the ummah. This is a vital necessity for the Islamic peoples, since in the past they have not enjoyed such balanced guidance all around. Some Islamic religious and spiritual leaders have been and are reasonable, saintly, and their interpretations of the Qur'an are correct, their applications, appropriate, while other such leaders have often incited the people to rage, violence, and destruction. Some have encouraged terrorist activity in the name of Islam. Can there by any doubt in this age that such behavior is beyond the pale of accepted norms of spiritual leadership in any tradition?

Some sort of universal assembly is required if Islam is to avoid fundamental erosion of its credibility and spiritual authenticity. A central authority is necessary to decide what is and what is not acceptable to the Islamic commonwealth, what is authentically Qur'anic and what is not, or what constitutes a distortion and even a perversion of Islamic teaching. It has become common to see these kinds of abuses, and when they occur, they cause serious damage to the reputation of Islam and Muslims. Something has to be done. Islamic spiritual leaders have to seize the initiative in history away from the extremists and assert themselves in a collective way, establishing a supreme authority in all matters pertaining to Islamic life.

Here I believe the Catholic Church can be of some precious assistance to our Muslim brothers and sisters. Through the contacts the Vatican has with religious and spiritual leaders in Islam, and through the contacts of national bishops' conferences, the Holy See could invite a good number of these leaders to the Vatican to have a consultation. The church leadership could offer its good offices to assist the Islamic leaders in exploring ways to establish such an assembly, discussing its nature, structure, composition, and authority. This is an enormously difficult task, and it's one that Islam and its leadership will have to do themselves; that's where the responsibility lies, but friends can help. The church can offer insight, resources, encouragement, and, of course, prayer. The role of the church here is as friend, supporter, guide, and inspiring voice for these leaders of Islam, who will be the real pioneers. The church can share its experience and the wisdom it has acquired through the centuries, especially associated with governance, relations with other powers, and diplomacy.

There is a lot of support in Islam for such an emergence of a central authority, but this authority must respect the traditional ways and the local authority of imams and Qur'anic scholars. The Islamic community around the world recognizes that something has to be done to protect the reputation of the ummah and the faith of the Islamic peoples. Negative forces that distort Islam and the Qur'an must not be allowed to control the future of the faith. A consensus must evolve among Muslim leaders on precisely how to proceed. The church can advise, inspire, share its experience, but it cannot decide for Islam. To reach a consensus, the ummah will have to listen to the most reasonable voices, the ones who are in dialogue with the rest of the world, with the conditions of modern life, with the Western cultures and their advanced understanding of ethnic and cultural diversity, democracy and tolerance, interfaith encounter and interreligious dialogue, with the possibility of genuine collaboration on projects that benefit the whole planet.

In contemporary Islam, countless voices are calling for reform, tolerance, and interfaith dialogue. They span the globe and are articulate representatives of an awakened consciousness to the larger picture beyond the ummah, with which the ummah must live in peace, converse, and find ways to work together for the benefit of all the human family. For instance, there is the remarkable Malaysian figure, Chandra Muzaffar, an activist, political scientist, progressive thinker, and founder of the Just World Trust, who is at the Centre for Civilization Dialogue in the University of Malaya, Kuala Lumpur, where he teaches, writes, and directs programs.[4] He is an eloquent spokesperson for an Islam in harmony with the other religions, modern life, and the movement toward universal responsibility, of which the Dalai Lama is the primary initiator.

Another very fascinating figure is the South African Muslim thinker Farid Esack, who is well known as an activist for human rights and reform and an impassioned scholar.[5] He has played a role in the struggle against apartheid in South Africa and is a leader in the interfaith movement, active in the Parliament of the World's Religions and the World Conference on Religion and Peace. He has been quite vocal in his criticism of political Islam, or the extremists, and just as critical of the negative aspects of U.S. power.

For example, Esack's commitment to justice in every situation is an absolute one, and he regards it as the basis of interfaith relations. He is convinced that praxis must take precedence over dialogue, or that the cause of justice and its pursuance in the interreligious context is the focus of such interfaith communication and collaboration. In his powerful work, *Qur'an, Liberation and Pluralism*, he observes prophetically:

> In the world today, interfaith solidarity for a just and human world is a far greater requirement than interfaith dialogue. It is good for us to understand the Other, to know about their beliefs and to understand where they come from. It is, however, only on the battlefield for human dignity for all of God's people, for freedom and justice, that we shall see and experience the point of our faith and what it actually does for us in our lives.[6]

This passage indicates the depth of passion and integrity of this important social activist, thinker, and spiritual leader. He and other such figures in contemporary Islam[7] within the ummah are persons with whom the Catholic Church should engage. It should promote their leadership and carry on a deep conversation for the good of Islam, the ummah, and, indeed, the world. It is clear that the ultimate goal of Farid Esack, and other such reformist thinkers, and the church is birthing a Civilization of Love, though their language is different. All the progressive figures in Islam want something similar to the church's vision, but they are expressing it through the values of the Qur'an and the unique terms of their respective disciplines and experience.

The Catholic Church, in its dialogue with Islam, can cultivate the great similarities of concern, born out of the compassionate heart of these two venerable faiths, who both are intensely focused on justice, peace, and a world that works for all people, not just an elite class. In its substantive conversations with the representatives of the ummah, church leaders can propose the goal of a Civilization of Love, a polity with a compassionate heart aflame with kindness, a universal society in which no one is left behind. The church can inspire Islam with a dream that everyone can share, a vision whose truth arises out of the eternal value of the Gospel.

THE CHURCH AS SACRAMENT OF RECONCILIATION

When the church—if the church—realizes its nature and role as the matrix, it will also become the sacrament of reconciliation for humankind in all its diversity. As matrix, it would a welcoming presence, a spaciousness of being that can bring the nations, cultures, and religions of the planet together. It can be the source of hope for all peoples, a vehicle of the Spirit in this terribly divided age fraught with unimaginable dangers and nearly superhuman challenges. If it incarnates divine Love as the presence of mercy in a time of such great suffering for the human family, other species, and the Earth itself, it can bring healing by being the sacrament of reconciliation, of bridging in itself the divisions of the world through its immense generosity.

To accomplish such a gigantic task of social construction, of civilization-building spanning millennia of cultures separated by geography and belief, by symbol, gesture, and mystical articulation, requires of the Catholic Church and its leadership a vast generosity as immense as the Divine itself. The church needs to think in larger terms than it has in the past, to let its spiritual imagination soar to the heights of seeing, conceiving, formulating, and manifesting in itself and the world. For this to happen, the church must embody the hope of all humanity. It must look beyond what it knows to embrace what it can become. What it is that it can become is present in the best of all the other great traditions of religion and spirituality. What it is to become is what it already inherently is: the living reality of God's *charitas*, which gives humanity its heart, its intrinsic motive power of growth, heroism, joy, and holiness.

This definitive nature of charitas, of divine love, what the Gospel calls *agape*, is the precious reality that has wrought the Catholic Church. The church has no choice but to immerse itself in its nature. The Spirit calls it in this new age to surrender to its nature as divine Love in this world. Its presence is necessary for the planet, but it must be a presence that is completely open to its deepest nature that rests in God's being, that is inspired by his charitas, his unfathomable spacious kindness. Most of all, if the church would truly follow the divine will for it in this troubled period of history, then it must trust the Spirit's inspiration, and not take refuge in the past, in the safe, in the familiar, in the old routine it knows so well. If the church will trust the Spirit, it will be led into greater freedom and much greater responsibility.

As the sacrament of reconciliation, as the living matrix, the church must surrender to divine Love totally! It cannot play it safe any longer, relying merely on its own all-too-human discretion. There is simply too much at stake. Like Christ, it must be that grain of wheat that dies and is buried and generates new life for the whole world. If the church can break out of its old habits that restrain it from moving into its larger identity, it can lead the planet into the new universal order of a civilization with a heart, a global order and society of love, divine Love transforming human love to a more fully enlightened form. The church, to achieve all of this, must walk humbly in fear and trembling, opening itself to the Spirit's prompting. It must not succumb to fear, for it is the hope of this Earth, and it cannot afford merely to observe and let others do it—that is, spark the transformation of consciousness on our planet. This is its sacred task, and the world will not make it without the church. Accepting its assignment as the matrix, as the sacrament of reconciliation, as the civilizational bridge builder, the Catholic Church can bring all the religions together in itself.

By embracing its destiny to be the catalyst of the Civilization of Love, the church will rely on its great gift of dialogue, but this gift is open-ended; there can be no strings attached. It is not one-sided and so is manipulated by the church for its own purposes. It must be genuinely available to the Spirit's purpose in the construction of the divine society that is meant to be for us all. Dialogue is a two-way street, and it must come out of our mutual vulnerability, the church's and the other religions, organizations, groups, persons. It cannot be controlled in its existential unfolding between conversants. Dialogue is a journey to a greater understanding that takes the interlocutors beyond their assumptions and propels them into an enlarged understanding of the shared Truth that encompasses their collective ontological or essential reality.

Out of such realizations arise areas of collaboration in practical life, the whole matters of justice, peace, reform of the global economic system in such ways that it works for everyone, and a commitment to environmental sustainability, which requires a system of economic philosophy and practice that protects the Earth and is sensitive to the needs of all segments of the global population, as well as the rights of other species, the necessity to guard these rights and promote biodiversity.

The church and the interfaith movement can call upon vast resources to advance the work of mutual understanding, harmony, and collaboration. Two can be identified here in terms of interreligious dialogue itself. These have grown out of actual dialogical encounters among members of the various traditions. Both of these examples have developed in the Catholic tradition or are inspired by it. These are *The Deep-Dialogue Decalogue: Ground Rules for Personal and Communal Deep-Dialogue* formulated by Leonard Swidler of the Global Dialogue Institute,[8] and *Points of Similarity Found in Dialogue*,[9] formulated by Abbot Thomas Keating and his Snowmass Conference.

The Deep-Dialogue Decalogue is a very practical document whose aim is to present wise guidelines for interreligious communication and between representatives of religion and science, in both an individual and communal context. These ground rules include ten basic insights that are the fruit of actual dialogical conversations that have evolved through trial and error with theory shedding light on the nature, process, and content of dialogue itself.

The First Ground Rule is "Be Open Within." This rule concerns an attitude of inner openness to learning from the other(s). The Second Ground Rule is "Attend, or Pay Attention." This means to be present to your dialogical partner and to yourself. The Third Ground Rule is "Be Open Between," and it requires an openness in each of the communities in the conversation and an openness between the communities. The Fourth Ground Rule involves "Honesty and Trust." It demands that each person arrives at the dialogue, and participates in it, with total honesty and utter sincerity. The Fifth Ground Rule advises the cultivation of "Personal Trust" through identifying common ground, while the Sixth Ground Rule says "Don't Prejudge; Compare Fairly." This means to be free of assumptions before the dialogue. The Seventh Ground Rule is "Define Yourself in

Dialogue." What this rule advocates is that each dialogue participant represents his or her own faith or position. The Eighth Ground Rule is very clear: "Treat Others as Equals." There has to be a real equality between the partners in conversation, so it is essential to treat each other as equals. The Ninth Ground Rule is "Be Healthily Self-Critical." We can only dare to criticize our partners in dialogue—not personally, of course—if we are self-critical about our tradition, our group in the process of dialogue, and ourselves. Finally, the Tenth Ground Rule is "Pass Over and Return." What this obscure ground rule aims at is the necessity of allowing yourself to experience the other's tradition or community "from within" and then to come back to your own changed or enriched. To experience "from within" means that it is not enough to either study or talk about another tradition or community; we must also experience it in its own terms. Having done this, or continuing to do so, will greatly expand understanding of our own tradition. These rules are conceived as ways to facilitate smooth and substantive conversations. They are very basic attitudes and practices.

On a deeper level are the *Points of Similarity Found in Dialogue* or, as they are also called, *Guidelines for Interreligious Understanding*. These points grew out of an existential process of years of dialogue by the fifteen members of the Snowmass Conference. All of the fifteen members are spiritual teachers in a world religion, and the Points of Similarity represent a consensus of agreement of the Snowmass Conference on matters of substance. The eight points are related to Ultimate Reality, faith, and spiritual life:

1. The world religions bear witness to the experience of Ultimate Reality to which they give various names: Brahman, Allah, [the] Absolute, God, [and] Great Spirit.
2. Ultimate Reality cannot be limited by any name or concept.
3. Ultimate Reality is the ground of infinite potentiality and actualization.
4. Faith is opening, accepting, and responding to Ultimate Reality. Faith in this sense precedes every belief system.
5. The potential for human wholeness—or in other frames of reference, enlightenment, salvation, transformation, blessedness, *nirvana*—is present in every human person.
6. Ultimate Reality may be experienced not only through religious practices, but also through nature, art, human relationships, and service of others.
7. As long as the human condition is experienced as separate from Ultimate Reality, it is subject to ignorance and illusion, weakness and suffering.

8. Disciplined practice is essential to the spiritual life; yet spiritual attainment is not the result of one's own efforts, but the result of the experience of oneness with Ultimate Reality.[10]

These guidelines or points are more on a theological level of dialogue, but they represent significant progress, an advance in what all the religions hold in common, or at least what some of their more enlightened members have arrived at through a depth of dialogue together over a number of years of conversation in the context of week-long retreats. In their annual retreat of May 1986, other points were agreed upon that involve service, virtue, and spiritual practice.[11]

These are only two examples of dialogical resources the Catholic Church can summon to its work. Ultimately, the primary goal of interreligious conversation, exchange, and collaboration is to serve the interests of the planet, and these interests are best served by following the papal dream of a Civilization of Love. That dream was articulated by Pope Paul VI and carried forth by Pope John Paul II. It has become part of the Catholic Church's mission. The Spirit has inspired this vision in the mind of these pontiffs, but perhaps they formulated the dream of the Earth itself, the hope of us all.

A Civilization of Love, a universal society animated by charitas, the selfless love incarnated in Christ's life, teachings, and actions, is the purpose of the Christian community around the world. Such a society will replace the old emphasis on power and an economic system that works for a minority of the human family. A society established in charitas is one whose kindness extends to all its members, especially the most vulnerable. It is this quality of selfless love, of agape, that the world must learn if it is to survive, just as it must learn the necessity and practice of nonviolence. The church is an agent of this consciousness; it is its heart, but it must be consistently informed by it, and allow itself to be renewed by its power and call. It is charitas that is the most humanizing resource humanity has, and the church can give this treasure to the world by first being an example of it itself. Its method of communicating it to the other religions and the whole of the human family is first by its example, and then by means of interreligious dialogue and its teaching. Humanity's hope is found in growth into this new civilizational ideal. Upon this ideal and its fruition, this enduring dream, may rest our very survival.

APPENDIX

Resources for Interreligious Dialogue and Collaboration

The information that follows is only a partial list, but more than adequate for anyone interested in further study, research, and facilitating a program in interfaith encounter. Although it is not exhaustive, it is indispensable to any kind of exploration of this area in the Catholic Church and its ongoing relations with the other religions or to understanding the interfaith phenomenon.

OFFICIAL CATHOLIC OFFICES

The Pontifical Council for Interreligious Dialogue
Via dell'Erba 1
00139 Rome, Italy
Phone: 011-379-69-88-43-21

Secretariat for Ecumenical and Interreligious Affairs
United States Conference of Catholic Bishops (USCCB)
3211 4th Street, N.E.
Washington, D.C. 20017
Phone: (202) 541-3000

Garland Pohl
President
National Association of Diocesan Ecumenical Officers
8003 Mobud Street
Houston, Texas 77036
Phone: (713) 774-0097

Each diocese and archdiocese has an ecumenical officer, who also responsible for interfaith relations. Please contact the chancery in your diocese for the appropriate official to obtain information on activities or to get advice on how to organize an event, a group, a class, or a parish program.

Monastic Interreligious Dialogue
Sister Mary Margaret Funk, O.S.B.
Our Lady of Grace Monastery
1402 Southern Avenue
Beech Grove, Indiana 46107
Phone: (317) 787-3287, ext. 3377

UNOFFICIAL CATHOLIC OFFICES

Father Thomas Keating, O.C.S.O.
The Snowmass Conference
St. Benedict's Monastery
1012 Monastery Road
Snowmass, Colorado 81654
Phone: (970) 927-3311

Sister Pascaline Coff, O.S.B.
Osage Monastery
18701 W. Monastery Road
Sand Springs, Oklahoma 74063
Phone: (918) 245-2734

Father Bruno Barnhart, O.S.B. Cam.
New Camaldoli Hermitage
Big Sur, California 93920
Phone: (831) 667-2456

INTERFAITH ORGANIZATIONS

World Conference on Religion and Peace (International Office)
777 UN Plaza
New York, New York 10017
Phone: (212) 687-2163
Website: www.wcrp.org

Council for a Parliament of the World's Religions
PO Box 1630
Chicago, Illinois 60690
(Office: 70 E. Lake, Chicago, Illinois 60601)
Phone: (312) 629-2990
Website: www.cpwr.org

United Religions Initiative
PO Box 29242
San Francisco, California 94129
Phone: (415) 561-2313
Website: www.united-religions.org

World Congress of Faiths
2 Market Street
Oxford, OX1 3EF
United Kingdom
Phone: 011-44-01-865-202-751
Website: www.worldfaiths.org

Temple of Understanding
720 5th Avenue
New York, New York 10019
Phone: (212) 246-2746
Website: http://templeofunderstanding.org

Fellowship of Reconciliation
Spoonstratt 38
1815 BK Alkmaar
Netherlands
Phone: 011-31-72-512-3014
Website: www. ifor.org

Graymoor Ecumenical & Interreligious Institute
Route 9, PO Box 300
Garrison, New York 10524
Phone: (914) 424-3671

International Association for Religious Freedom
2 Market Street
Oxford OX1 3EF
United Kingdom
Phone: 011-44-01-865-202-744
Website: www.iarf-religiousfreedom.net

Interfaith Center at the Presidio
2107 Van Ness Avenue, #300
San Francisco, California 04109
Phone: (415) 775-4635
Website: www.interfaith-presidio.org

Interfaith Conference of Metropolitan Washington
1426 9th Street, N.W.
Washington, D.C. 20001
Phone: (202) 324-6300
Website: www.interfaith-metrodc.org

Interfaith Council of Greater New York
20 Washington Square
Yonkers, New York 10019
Phone: (212) 627-7099

Interfaith Council of Montreal
2065 Sherbrooke Street W.
Montreal, Quebec H3H 1C6
Canada

InterFaith Network—UK
5–7 Tavisstock Place
London WC1H 9SN
United Kingdom
Phone: 011-44-71-388-0008
Website: www.interfaith.org.uk

USEFUL WEBSITES

American Academy of Religion: www.aarweb.org

Center for the Study of World Religions at Harvard University: www.hds.harvard.edu/cswr/index.html

Global Dialogue Institute: www.astro.temple.edu/~dialogue

Multifaith Institute: www.multifaith.net

Mysticism in the World's Religions: www.digiserve.com/mystic

North American Interfaith Network (NAIN): www.nain.org

World Interfaith Education Association (WIFEA): www.connect.ab.ca/~ifahlman/wifea.htm

NOTES

CHAPTER 1

1. A dream of Pope Paul VI during his pontificate.
2. The Parliament of the World's Religions promulgated a Global Ethic at the 1993 session in Chicago. See "Towards a Global Ethic: An Initial Declaration," in *Sourcebook of the World's Religions: An Interfaith Guide to Religion and Spirituality*, ed. Joel Beversluis (Novato, Calif.: New World Library, 2000), 174–82.
3. The commonwealth of Islamic peoples.

CHAPTER 2

1. For his life, see Vincent Cronin, *A Pearl to India: The Life of Roberto de Nobili* (New York: Dutton, 1959); and for his adaptation experiment, see Wayne Teasdale, *Bede Griffiths: An Introduction to His Interspiritual Vision* (Woodstock, Vt.: SkyLight Paths, 2003).
2. Cronin, *Pearl*, 70–71.
3. See B. Animananda, *The Blade: The Life and Work of Brahmabandhab Upadhyay* (Calcutta: Roy & Roy, 1945).
4. For background on Monchanin, see *In Quest of the Absolute: The Life and Works of Jules Monchanin*, ed. and trans. J. G. Weber (Kalamazoo, Mich.: Cistercian, 1977); and for Abhishiktananda, see M. M. Davy, *Swami Abhishiktananda: Le Passeur deux rives* (Paris: Cerf, 1981).
5. For his fascinating life before his move to India, see Bede Griffiths, *The Golden String: An Autobiography* (Springfield, Ill.: Templegate, 1980).
6. *Nostra Aetate* 1, in *The Documents of Vatican II*, ed. Walter M. Abbott, S.J. (New York: Guild, 1966), 660.
7. *Nostra Aetate* 2, 662–63.
8. *Nostra Aetate* 2, 662.
9. *Nostra Aetate*, see especially 4, 663–68.

10. See the Vatican's document, *We Remember: A Reflection on the Shoah*, available: www.vatican.va/roman_curia/pontifical_councils/chrstuni/documen.

11. Archbishop Francesco Gioia, "The Catholic Church and Other Religions," in *The Community of Religions: Voices and Images of the Parliament of the World's Religions*, ed. George Cairns and Wayne Teasdale (New York: Continuum, 1996), 83–90.

12. These two events were unique in historical terms because they brought a number of spiritual leaders together with the pope, on his initiative, for the first and second time in history in such a formal, global setting.

13. Gioia, "The Catholic Church," 86.

14. Pope Paul VI, *Ecclesiam Suam*, 85–86, in *Interreligious Dialogue: The Official Teaching of the Catholic Church (1963–1995)*, ed. Francesco Gioia (Boston: Pauline Books and Media; the Vatican: Pontifical Council for Interreligious Dialogue, 1997), 54–65.

15. Pope Paul VI, *Ecclesiam Suam*, 89, in *Interreligious Dialogue*, 65.

16. Pope Paul VI, *Ecclesiam Suam*, 92–95, in *Interreligious Dialogue*, 66–67.

17. Pope Paul VI, *Ecclesiam Suam*, 97, in *Interreligious Dialogue*, 68.

18. Pope Paul VI, *Ecclesiam Suam*, 99, in *Interreligious Dialogue*, 68.

19. Pope Paul VI, *Ecclesiam Suam*, 106, in *Interreligious Dialogue*, 70.

20. Pope Paul VI, *Ecclesiam Suam*, 106, in *Interreligious Dialogue*, 70–71.

21. Pope Paul VI, *Ecclesiam Suam*, 106, in *Interreligious Dialogue*, 71.

22. Pope Paul VI, *Ecclesiam Suam*, 112–13, *Dialogue*, 72.

23. Gioia, "The Catholic Church and Other Religions," 85.

24. *The Pope Speaks to India* (Bombay: St. Paul, 1986), 13, my emphasis.

25. "Discourse of the Pope to Zen and Christian Monks," *Bulletin* (Pontifical Council for Interreligious Dialogue), 23/1, no. 67 (1988): 5–6. This was a speech given to a group of Christian and Zen Buddhist monks participating in the Third East-West Spiritual Exchange.

26. For some background on the Synthesis Dialogues, consult the website www.synthesisdialogues.org.

27. *Paranirvana* is a term for the Ultimate state of consciousness, the Absolute Reality.

CHAPTER 3

1. This session was arranged by Dialog Inter Monasteres, a European association of Benedictines and Cistercians related to the Vatican's Pontifical Council for Interreligious Dialogue.

2. The Parliament of the World's Religions has greatly emphasized this kind of dialogue because agreement is more easily gotten. See its documents "Towards a Global Ethic: An Initial Declaration" and "A Call to Our Guiding Institutions," in *Sourcebook of the World's Religions*, ed. Beversluis, 174–82 (Global Ethic) and 184–201 (Call). The primary thrust of the parliament, and the in-

terfaith movement, is to meet around considerations of a practical nature, such as peace, justice, the environment, poverty, health care, the status of women, children, and refugees. In other words, the dialogue of the hands characterizes a considerable amount of the agenda in interfaith relations.

3. There is doubtless much good the religions do by themselves, but how much more effective they would be if they united their efforts.

4. The Interfaith Youth Core has an office at 1111 N. Wells Avenue, Suite 500, Chicago, Illinois 60610; e-mail: eboopatel@hotmail.com.

5. Write Play for Peace, 4750 N. Sheridan Road, Suite 225, Chicago, Illinois 60640; phone: (773) 275-0077; e-mail: info@playforpeace.org.

6. For more information, please contact the International Committee for the Peace Council, 2702 International Lane, Madison, Wisconsin 53704; phone: (608) 241-2209; website: www.peacecouncil.org.

7. See *Sourcebook of the World's Religions*, ed. Beversluis, 335–418, for contact information to many of these groups around the world.

8. See *Sourcebook of the World's Religions*, ed. Beversluis, 216–17; and Wayne Teasdale, *A Monk in the World: Cultivating a Spiritual Life* (Novato, Calif.: New World Library, 2002), 153–54.

9. MID is an association of North American Benedictines and Cistercians. The contact information is MID, 1402 Southern Avenue, Beach Grove, Indiana 46107-1197; phone: (317) 788-7581, ext. 3167; website: www.osb.org/mid.

10. Saccidananda Ashram on Shantivanam, the name of the grounds themselves, on the banks of the sacred river Kavery in Tannirpalli, near the city of Trichy in Tamil Nadu state, south India.

11. Write Rinchen Khando, Tibetan Nuns Project, Kashmir Cottage, Khara Danda Road (above Delek Hospital), Dharamsala 176215, District Kangra, Himachal Pradesh, India.

12. Hundred Acres Monastery (1964–1992) was a Cistercian or Trappist experiment inspired by Vatican II.

13. Inculturation refers to the Catholic Church's practice, after Vatican II, of expressing its liturgy, theology, and spirituality in local cultures where it finds itself.

14. This event was sponsored by Monastic Interreligious Dialogue. We will consider this significant group and its activities in chapter 8.

CHAPTER 4

1. Pope John Paul I, "Radio Message *Urbi et Orbi*" (Rome, August 27, 1978), in *Interreligious Dialogue,* ed. Gioia, 211.

2. Pope John Paul I, "To Participants at the Meeting of the European Committee of the World Conference of Religions for Peace" (Rome, September 30, 1978), in *Interreligious Dialogue,* ed. Gioia, 212. Notice the date is two days after the pope's death.

3. Now called the Pontifical Council for Interreligious Dialogue; this change was decreed by John Paul II in 1988.

4. Michael Fitzgerald, "Pope John Paul II and Interreligious Dialogue: A Catholic Assessment," in *John Paul II and Interreligious Dialogue*, ed. Byron Sherwin and Harold Kasimow (Maryknoll, N.Y.: Orbis, 1999), 207.

5. "*Redemptor Hominis*," March 4, 1979, in *Interreligious Dialogue,* ed. Gioia, pp. 87–89, related to interfaith matters.

6. Fitzgerald, "Pope John Paul II," 207.

7. "To the Plenary Session of the Pontifical Council for Interreligious," in *Interreligious Dialogue,* ed. Gioia, 501.

8. Fitzgerald, "Pope John Paul II," 219.

9. Fitzgerald, "Pope John Paul II," 219.

10. "To the Lay Monks of the Various Buddhist Schools," in *Interreligious Dialogue,* ed. Gioia, 219.

11. "To Representatives of Kenyan Hindus, Nairobi, May 7, 1980," in *Interreligious Dialogue,* ed. Gioia, 227–28.

12. "To the Young Muslims of Morocco, Casablanca, August 19, 1985," in *Interreligious Dialogue,* ed. Gioia, 303.

13. "To the Religious Authorities of India, February 3, 1986," in *Interreligious Dialogue,* ed. Gioia, 321–22.

14. "To the Religious Authorities of India," 322.

15. Fitzgerald, "Pope John Paul II," 219.

16. "Common Declaration Signed by Pope John Paul II and Ecumenical Patriarch Bartholomew I," in *Interreligious Dialogue*, ed. Gioia, 551.

17. "To Representatives of the World Council of Churches, Rome, April 11, 1986," in *Interreligious Dialogue*, ed. Gioia, 330.

18. "To Representatives of the World Council of Churches."

19. "To Representatives of the Jewish Community of Rome," in *Interreligious Dialogue*, ed. Gioia, 332.

20. "To Representatives of the Jewish Community of Rome," 332–33.

21. "To Representatives of the Jewish Community of Rome," 333, and *Nostra Aetate* 4.

22. "To Representatives of the Jewish Community of Rome," 333.

23. "To Representatives of the Jewish Community of Rome," 333–34.

24. "To Representatives of the Jewish Community of Rome," 334.

25. An *ad limina* visit is a canonical obligation of every bishop to report to the pope in person every five years by making their ad limina, or visit to the threshold of Peter—that is, the pope.

26. Gatherings of cardinals and bishops with the pope at the Vatican for discussions of special topics.

27. Fitzgerald, "Pope John Paul II," 208.

28. *Traditionalists* are a schismatic splinter organization who reject Vatican II and adhere to the directives of the Council of Trent, especially as regards the liturgy or the Latin mass in the Tridentine rite.

29. "To Representatives of Various Religions on the World Day of Prayer for Peace," in *Interreligious Dialogue*, ed. Gioia, 343.

30. "To Representatives of Various Religions on the World Day of Prayer for Peace," 344.

31. "To Representatives of Various Religions on the World Day of Prayer for Peace," 344–45.

32. "To Representatives of the Various Religions of the World at the Conclusion of the World Day of Prayer for Peace," in *Interreligious Dialogue*, ed. Gioia, 352.

33. Pope John Paul II, "Religion Has the Resources to Build Peace," *L'Osservatore Romano* 5 (1728), January 30, 2002, p. 6.

34. Pope John Paul II, "Religion Has the Resources to Build Peace."

35. Angelus Message: "Assisi: A Milestone toward a Civilization of Love," *L'Osservatore Romano* 5 (1728), 1.

36. His Holiness John Paul II, *Crossing the Threshold of Hope,* ed. Vittorio Messori (New York: Knopf, 1994).

37. John Paul II, *Crossing the Threshold of Hope*, 85.

38. John Paul II, *Crossing the Threshold of Hope*, 92.

39. John Paul II, *Crossing the Threshold of Hope*, 97.

40. John Paul II, *Crossing the Threshold of Hope*, 99.

CHAPTER 5

1. *Interreligious Dialogue*, ed. Gioia, 38.

2. *Nostra Aetate*, in *The Documents of Vatican II*, ed. Abbott, 38.

3. *Lumen Gentium*, in *The Documents of Vatican II*, ed. Abbott, 41.

4. *Nostra Aetate*, 40.

5. *Lumen Gentium*, 42.

6. *Lumen Gentium*, 42.

7. *Dignitatis Humanae*, in *The Documents of Vatican II*, ed. Abbott, 44–45.

8. *Dignitatis Humanae*, 46.

9. *Gaudium et Spes*, 3, 57, and *Lumen Gentium*, 48, complete text in *The Documents of Vatican II*, ed. Abbott, 79.

10. *The Documents of Vatican II*, 81, 60.

11. *Redemptoris Missio*, 176, in *The Documents of Vatican II*, ed. Abbott, 100.

12. *Redemptoris Missio*, 177, 101.

13. *Redemptoris Missio*, 177, 101.

14. *Catechism of the Catholic Church* 1, in *The Documents of Vatican II*, ed. Abbott, 104.

15. *Catechism of the Catholic Church* 2, in *The Documents of Vatican II*, ed. Abbott, 105.

16. *Catechism of the Catholic Church* 3, in *The Documents of Vatican II*, ed. Abbott, 106.

17. *Catechism of the Catholic Church* 3.

18. *Tertio Millennio Adveniente* 1, in *The Documents of Vatican II*, ed. Abbott, 108.

19. "To The Plenary Session of the Pontifical Council for Interreligious Dialogue," 1, in *The Documents of Vatican II*, ed. Abbott, 498.

20. *Dialogue and Proclamation*, 8, in *The Documents of Vatican II*, ed. Abbott, 611.

21. *Dialogue and Proclamation*,9, in *The Documents of Vatican II*, ed. Abbott, 611.

22. *Dialogue and Proclamation*, 10, in *The Documents of Vatican II*, ed. Abbott, 612.

23. *Dialogue and Proclamation*, 38, in *The Documents of Vatican II*, ed. Abbott, 621.

24. *Dialogue and Proclamation*, 47–50, in *The Documents of Vatican II*, ed. Abbott, 624–25.

25. *Dialogue and Proclamation*, 47, in *The Documents of Vatican II*, ed. Abbott, 624.

26. *Dialogue and Proclamation*, 48, in *The Documents of Vatican II*, ed. Abbott, 625.

27. *Dialogue and Proclamation*, 49, in *The Documents of Vatican II*, ed. Abbott, 625.

28. *Dialogue and Proclamation*, 50, in *The Documents of Vatican II*, ed. Abbott, 625.

29. *Dialogue and Proclamation*, 51, in *The Documents of Vatican II*, ed. Abbott, 626.

30. *Some Aspects of Christian Meditation*, 894, in *The Documents of Vatican II*, ed. Abbott, 592.

31. *Some Aspects of Christian Meditation*, 895, in *The Documents of Vatican II*, ed. Abbott, 593.

32. *Some Aspects of Christian Meditation*, 899, in *The Documents of Vatican II*, ed. Abbott, 595.

33. *Some Aspects of Christian Meditation*, 905, in *The Documents of Vatican II*, ed. Abbott, 598–99.

34. *Some Aspects of Christian Meditation*, 909, in *The Documents of Vatican II*, ed. Abbott, 600.

35. *Some Aspects of Christian Meditation*, 916, in *The Documents of Vatican II*, ed. Abbott, 603.

36. Also called simply *Dominus Iesus*. Consult the Vatican website for the entire document. When citing it here, I will refer to section numbers and not to pages, as is the custom with Catholic Church documents. Go to www.vatican .va/roman_curia/congregations/cfaith/documents/rc_con_cfaith_doc_200008 06_dominus-iesus_en.html.

37. *Dominus Iesus*, 4.

38. *Dominus Iesus*, 20.

39. *Dominus Iesus*, 22.

40. "To Representatives of the Jewish Community of Rome," 4, in *Interreligious Dialogue,* ed. Gioia, 334.

41. "To Representatives of the Jewish Community of Rome," 334.

42. "To Representatives of the Jewish Community of Rome," 334–35.

43. See the Vatican website, specifically www.vatican.va/roman_curia/pontifical_councils/chrstuni/documents/rc_pcchrstuni....

44. *Shoah* is the whole tragedy of the Holocaust.

45. Vatican's Commission for Religious Relations with the Jews, *We Remember: A Reflection on the Shoah* (Rome: Author, 1998), II.

46. Vatican's Commission for Religious Relations with the Jews, *We Remember,* 3; and *La Documentation Catholique* 29 (1938), col. 1460.

47. Vatican's Commission for Religious Relations with the Jews, *We Remember,* IV.

48. Vatican's Commission for Religious Relations with the Jews, *We Remember,* V; and Pope John Paul II, *Speech at the Synagogue of Rome,* April 13, 1986, 4: *Acta Apostolica Sedis* 78 (1986): 1120.

CHAPTER 6

1. For background on the adage *"extra ecclesiam nulla salus,"* I am relying on Jerome Theisen, *The Ultimate Church and the Promise of Salvation* (Collegeville, Minn.: St. John's University Press, 1976); and Joseph Osei-Bonsu, *"Extra Ecclesiam Nulla Salus:* Critical Reflections from Biblical and African Perspectives," in *Christianity and the Wider Ecumenism,* ed. Peter Phan (New York: Paragon, 1990).

2. The translation is taken from the Jerusalem Bible.

3. Osei-Bonsu, *"Extra Ecclesiam Nulla Salus,"* 132.

4. Osei-Bonsu, *"Extra Ecclesiam Nulla Salus,"* 132.

5. Clement of Alexandria, *The Tutor,* Bk. I, chap. 6, in *Patrologiae Cursus Completus, Series Graeca,* ed. J. P. Migne, 8, 281.

6. Origen, *Homilies on Joshua,* 3, 5, in *Patrologiae Cursus Completus, Series Graeca,* ed. J. P. Migne, 12, 841*f.*

7. Cyprian, Letter 69, 4, in *Corpus Scriptorum Ecclesiasticorum Latinorum* (Vienna: Gerold's, 1866), 3:753.

8. Cyprian, Letter 73, 21, in *Corpus Scriptorum Ecclesiasticorum Latinorum* 3:795.

9. Augustine, Letter 141, 5, in *Corpus Scriptorum Ecclesiasticorum Latinorum* 41:238.

10. Osei-Bonsu, *"Extra Ecclesiam Nulla Salus,"* 133.

11. Thomas Aquinas, *Summa Theologiae,* II–II, q. 2, a. 7, and 3.

12. H. Denzinger and A. Schonmetzer, eds., *Enchiridion et Definitionum de Rebus Fidei et Morum,* 33d ed. (Barcelona: Herder, 1965), 870. Hereafter this work is referred to as DS.

13. DS, 1351.

14. DS, 2865–67.

15. *Schema constitutionis dogmaticae de Ecclesia Christi Patrum examini proposi-tum: Acta et Decreta Sacrorum Conciliorum Recentiorum Collectio Lacensis,* Vol. VII (Freiburg: Herder, 1980), col. 569.

16. *Catechism of the Catholic Church,* 183, in *Interreligious Dialogue,* ed. Gioia, 106.

17. John Hick, "The Non-Absoluteness of Christianity," in *The Myth of Christian Uniqueness: Toward a Pluralistic Theology of Religions,* ed. John Hick and Paul Knitter, Faith Meets Faith Series (Maryknoll, N.Y.: Orbis, 1987), 21.

18. Gavin D'Costa, *Theology and Religious Pluralism* (New York: Blackwell, 1986), 80.

19. For some of these theologians in the early church who defended an in-clusive position, see Alan Race, *Christians and Religious Pluralism: Patterns in the Christian Theology of Religions* (Maryknoll, N.Y.: Orbis, 1982), 42–43.

20. Karl Rahner, "Christianity and the Non-Christian Religions," in *Christianity and Other Religions: Selected Readings,* ed. John Hick and Brian Hebble-thwaite (Philadelphia: Fortress Press, 1981), 61.

21. *Lumen Gentium, Dogmatic Constitution on the Church* 16, in *The Documents of Vatican II,* ed. Abbott, 35.

22. *Nostra Aetate* 2, in *Interreligious Dialogue,* ed. Gioia, 38.

23. John Paul II, *Dominum et Vivificantem,* 169–70, 96–97.

24. Karl Rahner, "Christianity and the Non-Christian Religions," in *Theo-logical Investigations,* vol. 5: *Later Writings,* trans. Karl Kruger (London: Darton, Longman & Todd, 1966), 123–31.

25. Rahner, "Christianity and the Non-Christian Religions," 118–31.

26. Brian Hebblethwaite, introduction, in *Christianity and Other Religions,* ed. Hick and Hebblethwaite, 8.

27. Paul Knitter, *One Earth, Many Faiths: Multifaith Dialogue and Global Responsibility* (Maryknoll, N.Y.: Orbis, 1995), 30.

28. Hick, "The Non-Absoluteness of Christianity," 23.

29. John Hick, *God Has Many Names* (Philadelphia: Westminister, 1980), 71.

30. Diana Eck, *Encountering God: A Spiritual Journey from Bozeman to Banaras* (Boston: Beacon, 1993), 191.

31. Eck, *Encountering God,* 192–93.

32. Eck, *Encountering God,* 193.

33. Eck, *Encountering God,* 193.

34. Eck, *Encountering God,* 196.

35. Eck, *Encountering God,* 196.

36. Eck, *Encountering God,* 198.

37. *Dominus Iesus,* 4.

38. Wolfhart Pannenberg, "Religious Pluralism and Conflicting Truth Claims," in *Christian Uniqueness Reconsidered,* ed. Gavin D'Costa (Maryknoll, N.Y.: Orbis, 1990), 97.

39. Jurgen Moltmann, "Is 'Pluralistic Theology' Useful for the Dialogue of World Religions?" in *Christian Uniqueness Reconsidered,* ed. D'Costa, 155.

CHAPTER 7

1. Cardinal Francis Arinze, *Meeting Other Believers: The Risks and Rewards of Interreligious Dialogue* (Huntington, Ind.: Our Sunday Visitor, 1998), 21–33.
2. Arinze, *Meeting Other Believers*, 35–42.
3. Arinze, *Meeting Other Believers*, 35–42.
4. Arinze, *Meeting Other Believers*, 43–54.
5. Pope John Paul II, *Redemptoris Missio* 3, in *Interreligious Dialogue*, ed. Gioia, 178.
6. Pope John Paul II, "To Religious Leaders of Sri Lanka, Colombo," in *Interreligious Dialogue*, ed. Gioia, 539–40.
7. Arinze, *Meeting Other Religions*, 16.
8. Arinze, *Meeting Other Religions*, 66.
9. José Pereira, "Epiphanies of Revelation," *Thought* 51, no. 201 (June 1976): 204.
10. Pereira, "Epiphanies of Revelation," 190.
11. Pereira, "Epiphanies of Revelation," 187.
12. Pereira, "Epiphanies of Revelation," 188. See also Andre Mehat, *Etudes sur les (Stromates) de Clement d'Alexandrie* (Paris: Seuil, 1966), especially 441.
13. Pereira, "Epiphanies of Revelation," 190.
14. Pereira, "Epiphanies of Revelation," 190.
15. Pereira, "Epiphanies of Revelation," 191.
16. See *Nicholai de Cusa de Pace Fidei cum Epistula ad Ioannem de Segoeia,* ed. R. Klibansky and H. Bascour (London: Warburg, 1956).
17. Pereira, "Epiphanies of Revelation," 192.
18. Pereira, "Epiphanies of Revelation," 195.
19. John Henry Newman, *An Essay on the Development of Christian Doctrine,* pt. 1, chap. 2, sect. 2, subsect. 5 (London: Longmans Green, 1906), 79.
20. Newman, *An Essay*, 89.
21. Pereira, "Epiphanies of Revelation," 204.
22. Paul Knitter, "Toward a Liberation Theology of Religions," in *The Myth of Christian Uniqueness: Toward a Pluralistic Theology of Religions*, ed. John Hick and Paul Knitter (Maryknoll, N.Y.: Orbis, 1987), 181.
23. Knitter, "Toward a Liberation Theology of Religions," 182–83.
24. Paul Knitter, *No Other Name? A Critical Survey of Christian Attitudes toward the World Religions*, American Society Missiology Series, no. 7 (Maryknoll, N.Y.: Orbis, 1986), 231.
25. Knitter, "Toward a Liberation Theology of Religions," 186.
26. Raimon Panikkar, *The Unknown Christ of Hinduism*, rev. ed. (Maryknoll, N.Y.: Orbis, 1981), 12.
27. Panikkar, *The Unknown Christ of Hinduism*, 25.
28. Raimon Panikkar, *The Trinity and the Religious Experience of Man* (Maryknoll, N.Y.: Orbis, 1973), 43.
29. "Comments of Francis X. Clooney," in *The Catholic Theological Society of America: Proceedings of the Fifty-Sixth Annual Convention*, vol. 56, June 7–10, 2001, Milwaukee, Wisconsin, 105.

30. "Comments of John Pawlikowski," in *The Catholic Theological Society of America: Proceedings of the Fifty-Sixth Annual Convention*, vol. 56, June 7–10, 2001, Milwaukee, Wisconsin, 98.

CHAPTER 8

1. Since this encounter has already been discussed, it will not be treated here.

2. For Merton's impressions of the Dalai Lama and a report on his three conversations with him, see *The Asian Journal of Thomas Merton*, ed. Naomi Burton, Patrick Hart, and James Laughlin (New York: New Directions, 1975), 100–125. He discusses other items and figures in this section as well.

3. Pascaline Coff, O.S.B., "How We Reached This Point: Communication Becoming Communion," in *The Gethsemani Encounter: A Dialogue on the Spiritual Life by Buddhist and Christian Monastics*, ed. Donald W. Mitchell and James A. Wiseman, O.S.B. (New York: Continuum, 1997), 4–5.

4. See *A SourceBook of the Earth's Community of Religions*, ed. Joel Beversluis (Grand Rapids, Mich.: CoNexus, 1995), 171.

5. *A SourceBook of the Earth's Community of Religions*, 131–37.

6. *A SourceBook of the Earth's Community of Religions*, 171.

7. *The Gethsemani Encounter*, xxi.

8. *The Gethsemani Encounter*, xxi.

9. *The Gethsemani Encounter*, 170–255.

10. *The Gethsemani Encounter*, 257–61.

11. *The Gethsemani Encounter*, 261–77.

12. *The Gethsemani Encounter*, 19–33.

13. *The Gethsemani Encounter*, 22.

14. *The Gethsemani Encounter*, 26–27.

15. *The Gethsemani Encounter*, 28.

16. *The Gethsemani Encounter*, 28–31.

17. *The Gethsemani Encounter*, 32.

18. *The Gethsemani Encounter*, 79.

19. *The Gethsemani Encounter*, 119.

20. *The Gethsemani Encounter*, 122.

21. "The Spiritual Guide," in *The Gethsemani Encounter*, 126.

22. *The Gethsemani Encounter*, xxii.

23. The report was published as "Gethsemani II," *Monastic Interreligious Dialogue Bulletin* 69 (September 2002). The proceedings appeared in print as *Transforming Suffering: Reflections on Finding Peace in Troubled Times*, ed. Donald W. Mitchell and James A. Wiseman, O.S.B. (New York: Doubleday, 2003).

24. "Gethsemani II," 1.

25. "Gethsemani II," 2.

26. "Gethsemani II," 2.

27. "Gethsemani II," 2.

28. Thomas Ryan, "Catholic and Buddhist Monastics Focus on Suffering: A Report on the Gethsemani II Encounter," *International Bulletin of Monastic Interreligious Dialogue Commissions* 13, no. 1 (2002): 11.

29. Ryan, "Catholic and Buddhist Monastics," 12.

30. "Gethsemani II," 4.

31. For some history of this dialogue on a deep existential level, see my *Bede Griffiths: An Introduction to His Interspiritual Thought* (Woodstock, Vt.: SkyLight Paths, 2003), chap. 2.

32. Teasdale, *Bede Griffiths*, 24–28.

33. Teasdale, *Bede Griffiths*, 28–32.

34. Teasdale, *Bede Griffiths*, 32–37.

35. See, for example, his masterpiece, *Saccidananda: A Christian Approach to Advaitic Experience*, rev. ed. (Delhi: ISPCK, 1984).

36. *Saccidananda: A Christian Approach to Advaitic Experience*, rev. ed., 48.

CHAPTER 9

1. Liberation theology has also played a role in educating the church about these dimensions of empowerment, often borrowing tools of analysis from Marxism, rather than from the Gospel. It seems this tendency has been rectified in the light of ecclesial criticism of such an easy reliance on the Marxist critique, which often vitiates the more powerful perspective of Christ. In any case, the church has to address all types of oppression, supporting programs to transform them.

2. In terms of ecological responsibility and justice, see Thomas Berry, *The Dream of the Earth* (San Francisco: Sierra Club Books, 1988); Thomas Berry, with Brian Swimm, *The Universe Story: From the Primordial Flaring Forth to the Ecozoic Era. A Celebration of the Unfolding of the Cosmos* (San Francisco: Harper-San Francisco, 1992); and Thomas Berry, *The Great Work: Our Way into the Future* (New York: Bell Tower, 1999). Berry is without question the most eloquent voice on the planet for an understanding of the mystical roots of environmental awareness. He combines a comprehensive grasp of ecology with a living nature-mysticism that is breath-taking.

3. See *Sourcebook of the World's Religions*, ed. Beversluis, 262–64.

4. *Sourcebook of the World's Religions*, ed. Beversluis, 174–82.

5. *Sourcebook of the World's Religions*, ed. Beversluis, 184–201.

6. *Sourcebook of the World's Religions*, ed. Beversluis, 216–17.

CHAPTER 10

1. For a good discussion of some of the issues involved, see *Subverting Greed: Religious Perspectives on the Global Economy*, ed. Paul F. Knitter and Chandra Muzaffar (Maryknoll, N.Y.: Orbis and Boston Research Center for the 21st Century, 2002).

2. *Nicholas of Cusa on Religious Harmony: Text, Concordance and Translation of De Pace Fidei*, trans. James E. Biechler, *Texts and Studies in Religion*, vol. 55 (Lewiston, N.Y.: Mellen, 1990).

3. *Nicholas of Cusa*, sec. 1, 4.

4. See Chandra Muzaffar, *Rights, Religion and Reform: Enhancing Human Dignity through Spiritual and Moral Transformation* (New York: Routledge, 2002); with Sulak Sivaraksa, *Alternative Politics for Asia: A Buddhist-Muslim Dialogue* (New York: Lantern, 2003); and "Universalism in Islam," in *Liberal Islam: A SourceBook*, ed. Charles Kurzman (New York: Oxford University Press, 1998).

5. See Farid Esack, *Qur'an, Liberation and Pluralism: An Islamic Perspective of Interreligious Solidarity against Oppression* (Oxford: Oneworld, 2002), and *On Being a Muslim: Finding a Religious Path in the World Today* (Oxford: Oneworld, 2002).

6. Esack, *Qur'an*, 258.

7. See also *The Place of Tolerance in Islam*, ed. Khaled Abou El Fadl (Boston: Beacon, 2002), and *Progressive Muslims: On Justice, Gender, and Pluralism*, ed. Omid Safi (Oxford: Oneworld, 2003).

8. Leonard Swidler, *The Deep-Dialogue Decalogue*, in *Sourcebook of the World's Religions*, ed. Beversluis, 138–41.

9. Thomas Keating, "*Points of Similarity Found in Dialogue*," in *Sourcebook of the World's Religions*, ed. Beversluis, 137–38.

10. Keating, "*Points of Similarity*," 137.

11. Keating, "*Points of Similarity*," 137–38.

BIBLIOGRAPHY

This bibliography represents books cited in this text and recommended readings not mentioned previously. Obviously the list is not exhaustive, but more than sufficient to study interreligious dialogue, engage in existential encounter, and acquire ideas and direction for group reading and discussions, visits to sites, and contact with interfaith organizations.

Abbott, Walter M., ed. *The Documents of Vatican II*. New York: Guild, 1966.

Abhiskitananda. *Saccidananda: A Christian Approach to Advaitic Experience*. Rev. ed. Delhi: ISPCK, 1984.

Angelus Message. "Assisi: A Milestone toward a Civilization of Love." *L'Osservatore Romano* 5 (1728), January 30, 2002, pp. 1, 12.

Animananda, B. *The Blade: The Life and Work of Brahmabandhab Upadhyay*. Calcutta: Roy & Roy, 1945.

Aquinas, Thomas. "Summa Theologiae." In *The Basic Writings of Saint Thomas Aquinas*, ed. Anton C. Pegis. 2 vols. New York: Random House, 1945.

Arinze, Cardinal Francis. *Meeting Other Believers: The Risks and Rewards of Interreligious Dialogue*. Huntingdon, Ind.: Our Sunday Visitor, 1998.

Berry, Thomas. *The Dream of the Earth*. San Francisco: Sierra Club, 1988.

———. *The Great Work: Our Way into the Future*. New York: Bell Tower, 1999.

Berry, Thomas, with Brian Swimm. *The Universe Story: From the Primordial Flaring Forth to the Ecozoic Age. A Celebration of the Unfolding of the Cosmos*. San Francisco: HarperSanFrancisco, 1992.

Beversluis, Joel, ed. *A SourceBook of the Earth's Community of Religions*. Grand Rapids, Mich.: CoNexus, 1995.

———, ed. *Sourcebook of the World's Religions: An Interfaith Guide to Religion and Spirituality*. Novato, Calif.: New World Library, 2000.

Biechler, James E., trans. *Nicholas of Cusa on Religious Harmony: Text, Concordance and Translation of De Pace Fidei*. Texts and Studies in Religion, vol. 55. Lewiston, N.Y.: Mellen, 1990.

Burton, Naomi, Patrick Hart, and James Laughlin, eds. *The Asian Journal of Thomas Merton.* New York: New Directions, 1975.

Clement of Alexandria. *The Tutor,* Bk. I, chap. 6. In *Patrologiae Cursus Completus, Series Graeca,* ed. J. P. Migne (Paris: Carnier and Migne, 1886), 8, 281.

Coff, Pascaline. "How We Reached This Point: Communication Becoming Communion." In *The Gethsemani Encounter: A Dialogue on the Spiritual Life by Buddhist and Christian Monastics,* ed. Donald W. Mitchell and James A. Wiseman. New York: Continuum, 1997.

"Comments of Francis X. Clooney." In *The Catholic Theological Society of America: Proceedings of the Fifty-Sixth Annual Convention,* vol. 56, June 7–10, 2001, Milwaukee, Wisconsin.

Cronin, Vincent. *A Pearl to India: The Life of Roberto de Nobili.* New York: Dutton, 1959.

Cyprian. *Corpus Scriptorum Ecclesiasticorum Latinorum.* Vol. 3. Vienna: Gerold's, 1866.

Davy, M. M. *Swami Abhishiktananda: Le Passeur deux rives.* Paris: Cerf, 1981.

D'Costa, Gavin. *Theology and Religious Pluralism.* New York: Basil, 1986.

———, ed. *Christian Uniqueness Reconsidered.* Maryknoll, N.Y.: Orbis, 1990.

Denzinger, H., and A. Schonmetzer, eds. *Enchiridion et Definitionum de Rebus Fidei et Morum.* 33d ed. Barcelona: Herder, 1965.

"Discourse of the Pope to Zen and Christian Monks." *Bulletin* (Pontifical Council for Interreligious Dialogue), 23/1, no. 67 (1988): 5–6.

Eck, Diana. *Encountering God: A Spiritual Journey from Bozeman to Banaras.* Boston: Beacon, 1993.

El Fadl, Khaled Abou, ed. *The Place of Tolerance in Islam.* Boston: Beacon, 2002.

Esack, Farid. *On Being a Muslim: Finding a Religious Path in the World Today.* Oxford: Oneworld, 2002.

———. *Qur'an, Liberation and Pluralism: An Islamic Perspective of Interreligious Solidarity against Oppression.* Oxford: Oneworld, 2002.

Fitzgerald, Michael. "Pope John Paul II and Interreligious Dialogue: A Catholic Assessment." In *John Paul II and Interreligious Dialogue,* ed. Byron Sherwin and Harold Kasimow. Maryknoll, N.Y.: Orbis, 1999.

"Gethsemani II." *Monastic Interreligious Dialogue Bulletin* 69 (September 2002).

Gioia, Archbishop Francesco. "The Catholic Church and Other Religions." In *The Community of Religions: Voices and Images of the Parliament of the World's Religions,* ed. Wayne Teasdale and George F. Cairns. New York: Continuum, 1996.

———. *Interreligious Dialogue: The Official Teaching of the Catholic Church (1963–1995).* Rome: Pontifical Council for Interreligious Dialogue, and Boston: Pauline Books & Media, 1997.

Griffiths, Bede. *The Golden String: An Autobiography.* Rev. ed. Springfield, Ill.: Templegate, 1980.

Hick, John. *God Has Many Names.* Philadelphia: Westminister, 1980.

————. "The Non-Absoluteness of Christianity." In *The Myth of Christian Uniqueness: Toward a Pluralistic Theology of Religions*, ed. John Hick and Paul Knitter. Faith Meets Faith Series. Maryknoll, N.Y.: Orbis, 1987.

Hick, John, and Brian Hebblethwaite, eds. *Christianity and Other Religions: Selected Readings*. Philadelphia: Fortress, 1981.

Hick, John, and Paul Knitter, eds. *The Myth of Christian Uniqueness: Toward a Pluralistic Theology of Religions*. Maryknoll, N.Y.: Orbis, 1988.

John Paul II. *Crossing the Threshold of Hope*, ed. Vittorio Messori. New York: Knopf, 1994.

————. "Religion Has the Resources to Build Peace." *L'Osservatore Romano* 5 (1728), January 30, 2002, p. 6.

————. *Speech at the Synagogue of Rome,* April 13, 1986. 4: *Acta Apostolica Sedis* 78 (1986): 1120.

Kasimow, Harold, and Byron Sherwin, eds. *John Paul II and Interreligious Dialogue*. Maryknoll, N.Y.: Orbis, 1999.

Keating, Thomas. "Points of Similarity Found in Dialogue." In *Sourcebook of the World's Religions*, ed. Joel Beversluis. Novato, Calif.: New World Library, 2000.

Klibansky, R., and H. Bascour, eds. *Nicholai de Cusa de Pace Fidei cum Epistula ad Ioannem de Segoeia*. London: Warburg, 1956.

Knitter, Paul. *God Has Many Names*. Philadelphia: Westminister, 1980.

————. *No Other Name: A Critical Survey of Christian Attitudes toward the World Religions*. American Society Missiology Series, No. 7. Maryknoll, N.Y.: Orbis, 1986.

————. *One Earth, Many Faiths: Multifaith Dialogue and Global Responsibility*. Maryknoll, N.Y.: Orbis, 1995.

————. "Toward a Liberation Theology of Religions." In *The Myth of Christian Uniqueness: Toward a Pluralistic Theology of Religions*, ed. John Hick and Paul Knitter. Maryknoll, N.Y.: Orbis, 1987.

Knitter, Paul, and Chandra Muzaffar, eds. *Subverting Greed: Religious Perspectives on the Global Economy*. Maryknoll, N.Y.: Orbis and Boston Research Center for the 21st Century, 2002.

Lumen Gentium. In *The Documents of Vatican II*, ed. Walter M. Abbott. New York: Guild, 1966.

Mehat, Andre. *Etudes sur les (Stromates) de Clement d'Alexandrie*. Paris: Editions du Seuil, 1966.

Mitchell, Donald W., and James A. Wiseman. *The Gethsemani Encounter: A Dialogue on the Spiritual Life by Buddhist and Christian Monastics*. New York: Continuum, 1997.

Muzaffar, Chandra. *Rights, Religion and Reform: Enhancing Human Dignity through Spiritual and Moral Transformation*. New York: Routledge, 2002.

————. "Universalism in Islam." In *Liberal Islam: A SourceBook*, ed. Charles Kurzman. New York: Oxford University Press, 1998.

Muzaffar, Chandra, with Sulak Sivaraksa. *Alternative Politics for Asia: A Buddhist-Muslim Dialogue*. New York: Lantern, 2003.

Newman, John Henry. *An Essay on the Development of Christian Doctrine.* London: Longmans Green, 1906.

Nicholai de Cusa de Pace Fidei cum Epistula ad Ioannem de Segoeia, ed. R. Klibansky and H. Bascour. London: Warburg, 1956.

Nostra Aetate. In *The Documents of Vatican II,* ed. Walter M. Abbott. New York: Guild, 1966.

Origen. *Homilies on Joshua.* In *Patrologiae Cursus Completus, Series Graeca,* ed. J. P. Migne, 12.

Osei-Bonsu, Joseph. *"Extra Ecclesiam Nulla Salus:* Critical Reflections from Biblical and African Perspectives." In *Christianity and the Wider Ecumenism,* ed. Peter Phan. New York Paragon, 1990.

Panikkar, Raimon. *The Trinity and the Religious Experience of Man.* Maryknoll, N.Y.: Orbis, 1973.

———. *The Unknown Christ of Hinduism.* Maryknoll, N.Y.: Orbis, 1981.

Pannenberg, Wolfhart. "Religious Pluralism and Conflicting Truth Claims." In *Christian Uniqueness Reconsidered,* ed. Gavin D'Costa. Maryknoll, N.Y.: Orbis, 1990.

Parliament of the World's Religions. "A Call to Our Guiding Institutions." In *Sourcebook of the World's Religions,* ed. Joel Beversluis. Novato, Calif.: New World Library, 2000.

———. "Towards a Global Ethic: An Initial Declaration." In *Sourcebook of the World's Religions,* ed. Joel Beversluis. Novato, Calif.: New World Library, 2000.

Pereira, José. "Epiphanies of Revelation." *Thought* 51, no. 201 (June 1976).

The Pope Speaks to India. Bombay: St. Paul, 1986.

Race, Alan. *Christians and Religious Pluralism: Patterns in the Christian Theology of Religions.* Maryknoll, N.Y.: Orbis, 1892.

Rahner, Karl. "Christianity and the Non-Christian Religions." *Theological Investigations.* Vol. 5: *Later Writings.* Trans. Karl Kruger. London: Darton, Longman & Todd, 1966.

Ryan, Thomas. "Catholic and Buddhist Monastics Focus on Suffering: A Report on the Gethsemani II Encounter." *International Bulletin of Monastic Interreligious Dialogue Commissions* 13, no. 1 (2002): 11.

Safi, Omid. *Progressive Muslims: On Justice, Gender, and Pluralism.* Oxford: Oneworld, 2003.

Schema constitutionis dogmaticae de Ecclesia Christi Patrum examini propositum: Acta et Decreta Sacrorum Conciliorum Recentiorum Collectio Lacensis. Vol. VII. Freiburg: Herder, 1980.

Swidler, Leonard. "The Deep-Dialogue Decalogue." In *Sourcebook of the World's Religions,* ed. Joel Beversluis. Novato, Calif.: New World Library, 2000.

Teasdale, Wayne. *Bede Griffiths: An Introduction to His Interspiritual Thought.* Woodstock, Vt.: SkyLight Paths, 2003.

———. *A Monk in the World: Cultivating a Spiritual Life.* Novato, Calif.: New World Library, 2002.

Theisen, Jerome. *The Ultimate Church and the Promise of Salvation*. Collegeville, Minn.: St. John's University Press, 1976.

Weber, J. G. *In Quest of the Absolute: The Life and Works of Jules Monchanin*. Kalamazoo, Mich.: Cistercian, 1977.

RECOMMENDED READING

Cornille, Catherine, ed. *Many Mansions? Multiple Religious Belonging and Christian Identity*. Maryknoll, N.Y.: Orbis, 2002.

Coward, Harold. *Pluralism: Challenge to World Religions*. Maryknoll, N.Y.: Orbis, 1985.

Dupuis, Jacques. *Christianity and the Religions: From Confrontation to Dialogue*. Trans. Phillip Berryman. Maryknoll, N.Y.: Orbis, 2001.

Henry, Patrick, ed. *Benedict's Dharma: Buddhists Reflect on the Rule of Saint Benedict*. New York: Riverhead, 2001.

Kurzman, Charles, ed. *Liberal Islam: A Sourcebook*. New York: Oxford University Press, 1998.

Panikkar, R. *The Intra-Religious Dialogue*. New York: Paulist, 1978.

———. *Invisible Harmony: Essays on Contemplation and Responsibility*. Minneapolis: Fortress, 1995.

Teasdale, Wayne. *The Mystic Heart: Discovering a Universal Spirituality in the World's Religions*. Novato, Calif.: New World Library, 1999.

Teasdale, Wayne, and George F. Cairns, eds. *The Community of Religions: Voices and Images of the Parliament of the World's Religions*. New York: Continuum, 1996.

Walker, Susan, ed. *Speaking of Silence: Christians and Buddhists on the Contemplative Way*. Mahwah, N.J.: Paulist, 1987.

JOURNALS

Journal of Ecumenical Studies
Interreligious Insight: A Journal of Dialogue and Engagement
Monastic Interreligious Dialogue Bulletin

INDEX

Cyprian, 84

Dalai Lama: on Gethsemani
Encounter I, 125; "Harmony,
Dialogue and Meditation," 123;
on interreligious dialogue, 23, 28,
115, 117–18; interreligious
friendships, 20, 34, 43–44, 140; on
nonviolence, 31; "Spiritual
Guidance and the Attainment of
Nirvana," 124–25; "The Path to
Calm Abiding," 123–24; tribute to
Thomas Merton, 121
D'Costa, Gavin, *Theology and
Religious Pluralism,* 88
Declaration on the Relationship of
the Church to Non-Christian
Religions (Paul VI). *See Nostra
Aetate*
The Deep-Dialogue Decalogue
(Swidler), 161–62
deicide, 51
democracy, 3, 151
de Nobili, Roberto, 10, 127
Desert Fathers, 9
dialogue, 4–6, 68–69, 160–61; aims
of, 35–36; ground rules, 19–22,
27, 67, 70, 161–62; method of, 35
dialogue, intermonastic, 6, 23–24, 35,
46. *See also* Gethsemani Encounter
I; Gethsemani Encounter II;
Intermonastic Dialogue Exchange;
Intermonastic Hospitality Program
dialogue, interreligious, 5–7, 24–27,
34–37, 44, 65, 96; Catholic
Church's contributions to, 6–7,
46, 53–57; within the community
of religions, 142; and
evangelization, 15–18, 24, 42,
62–63, 70, 100–103, 107; as
mutual fecundation, 110; obstacles
to, 70–71; Paul VI's teachings on,
15–18, 26; pre-Vatican II, 9–11;

resources for, 165–69; Vatican II,
12–15
Dialogue and Proclamation (PCID and
Congregation for Evangelization
of Peoples), 68–70, 102
dialogue of friendship, 28, 33–34
dialogue of life, 28–30, 33, 72, 143
dialogue of play, 31
dialogue of salvation, 16, 67–68, 103
dialogue of the hands, 28, 30–33,
172–73n2
dialogue of the head, 28
dialogue of the heart, 28–29, 72
Dignitatis Humanae (Vatican II), 64
direct revelation, 106
diversity, 20, 95, 142, 151
divine love, 160, 163
divine providence, 85
divinity, 123
Dogmatic Constitution on the Church, 63
Dominum et Vivificantm (John Paul II),
90–91
Dominus Iesus (CDF), 74–76, 87, 91,
97, 112–13, 143

Earth, responsibility for, 26
Ecclesiam Suam (Paul VI), 15–16
Eck, Diana, *Encountering God,* 94–96
ecology, 137
economic polarization, 3, 30, 139,
151, 153, 161
emptiness, 35
Encountering God (Eck), 94–96
encyclicals, 15
entertainment media, promoting
violence, 138
environment, 137, 150, 153, 161
"Epiphanies of Revelation" (Pereira),
103–6
Esack, Farid, *Qur'an, Liberation and
Pluralism,* 158
ethical guidelines. *See* moral values
Eucharist, 99

ABOUT THE AUTHOR

Wayne Teasdale is a Christian monk in two traditions: Catholic and Indian sannyasa (renunciation). He was initiated as a Christian into Indian sannyasa by Dom Bede Griffiths, O.S.B. in India in January 1989, and took final vows as a monk under the Archbishop of Chicago in August 2003. He earned a doctorate in theology from Fordham University, and is an adjunct professor of spirituality, comparative religion, and ethics at Catholic Theological Union, DePaul University, and Columbia College. He is the author of several books, including *The Mystic Heart*, *A Monk in the World*, and *Bede Griffiths: An Introduction to his Interspiritual Thought*, and hundreds of articles. He was a member of Monastic Interreligious Dialogue for several years, and serves on the board of the Parliament of the World's Religions in Chicago.